Reproducible Activities

Building Grammar

Teaching the Basics One Skill at a Time

Grades 7-8

By
Rhonda Chapman

Cover Illustration by
Matthew Van Zomeren

Inside Illustrations by
Dave Winter

Published by Instructional Fair • TS Denison
an imprint of

McGraw-Hill
Children's Publishing

About the Author

Rhonda Chapman is a graduate of Grand Valley State University where she received degrees in special education, elementary education, and reading. She has 13 years experience in the classroom as well as home schooling and private tutoring. Rhonda has written many books for McGraw-Hill Children's Publishing, including *Skills for Young Writers* for grade 6 and *Reading Comprehension* for grade 5.

Credits

Author: Rhonda Chapman
Cover Graphics: Matthew Van Zomeren
Inside Illustrations: Dave Winter
Project Director/Editor: Sara Bierling
Editors: Meredith Van Zomeren, Wendy Roh Jenks
Page Production: Pat Geasler

McGraw-Hill
Children's Publishing
A Division of The McGraw-Hill Companies

Published by Instructional Fair • TS Denison
An imprint of McGraw-Hill Children's Publishing

Send all inquiries to:
McGraw-Hill Children's Publishing
3195 Wilson Drive NW
Grand Rapids, Michigan 49544

Building Grammar—grades 7-8
ISBN: 1-56822-911-9

Table of Contents

parts of speech

Name ______________________

Working Words

> Many words act as various parts of speech depending on their use in a sentence.
>
> ***work***
>
> *I really enjoy my* ***work****.* (noun)
>
> *Mr. James assembled the* ***work*** *force.* (adjective)
>
> *Most people* ***work*** *hard to earn a living.* (verb)

Identify the part of speech of each boldfaced word: **N** (noun), **V** (verb), **ADJ** (adjective), or **ADV** (adverb).

_____ 1. Read a **book** just for fun.

_____ 2. It's important to **book** your reservations well in advance.

_____ 3. The **book** cover protects the old classic.

_____ 4. **Duck** before you get hit!

_____ 5. He used a **duck** call to attract the flying fowl.

_____ 6. **Ducks** rest in the reeds by the pond.

_____ 7. Living in the country, we drink **well** water.

_____ 8. Our **well** has never run dry.

_____ 9. Drink lots of water, and you will feel **well**.

_____ 10. That was a **wrong** turn in the opposite direction.

_____ 11. Can you learn to overlook a **wrong**?

_____ 12. She had been **wronged**.

_____ 13. The clouds are heavy with **rain**.

_____ 14. It **rained** cats and dogs all day long.

_____ 15. The **rain** forests are very important natural resources.

Using the parts of speech given, write sentences for the word **trick**.

(noun) 1. ______________________________

(adjective) 2. ______________________________

(verb) 3. ______________________________

Name ______________________

Hanukkah

noun—person, place, or thing	**adverb**—modifies a verb
adjective—modifies a noun	**article**—a, an, the (modify nouns)
preposition—relates a noun or pronoun to another	**pronoun**—can be singular, plural, or possessive; takes the place of a noun
conjunction—links two or more words or groups of words	**interjection**—a word or phrase used in exclamation to express emotion
verb—shows action or a state of being	

Read the narrative below and determine the part of speech of the word that follows each number. Write the part of speech from the box above on the corresponding line below.

My family observes Hanukkah, an 1.important holiday celebrated by the Jewish people. It 2.begins each year on the twenty-fifth day of the Hebrew month of Kislev 3.and lasts eight days. 4.Hanukkah usually falls 5.in December.

Hanukkah 6.is called the Feast of Lights. One important symbol of the 7.holiday is the *menorah.* A menorah is a candlestick with 8.nine cups for candles. The ninth cup holds the *shamash* 9.candle. Each night of Hanukkah 10.my father lights the shamash candle 11.first and uses it 12.to light the other candles. One candle is lit 13.each night 14.until the final night of Hanukkah.

Hanukkah is 15.a time of gift giving and game playing too. The children 16.receive gifts and sing songs. 17.Wow, can you believe we children sometimes get money during Hanukkah? One of my favorite things to do is play with the dreidel, which is used to play games during the 18.holiday. The dreidel is a 19.toplike toy with a Hebrew letter 20.inscribed on each side.

During Hanukkah, we 21.joyously celebrate the history of our people and our religion.

1. ________	8. ________	15. ________
2. ________	9. ________	16. ________
3. ________	10. ________	17. ________
4. ________	11. ________	18. ________
5. ________	12. ________	19. ________
6. ________	13. ________	20. ________
7. ________	14. ________	21. ________

Name ______________________________

Yikes!

> An **interjection** is a word that is used alone to express strong emotions.
>
> *Wow!, Oh!, Whew!, Hey!*

Supply an interjection for each of the comics below.

Interjection Bank

ah	aha	fine	gosh	hey	huh
never	oh	oops	ouch	sh	ugh
psst	great	wow	whew	what	

_______ ! Bring that back!

_______ ! That's gross!

_______ ! Did I do that?

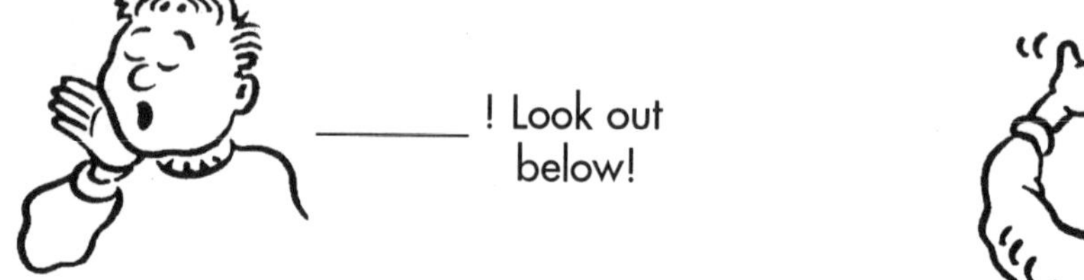

_______ ! Look out below!

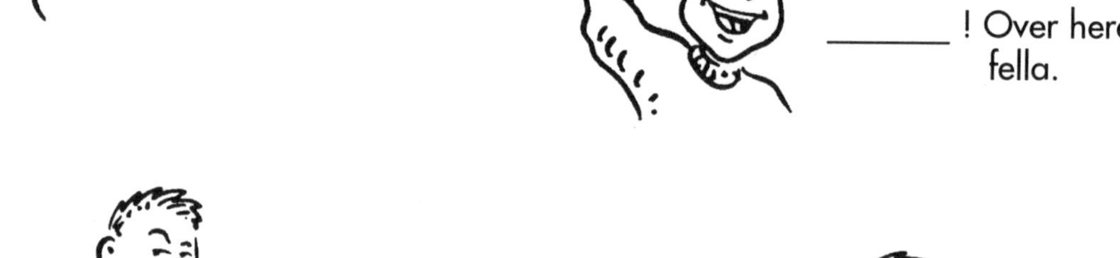

_______ ! Over here fella.

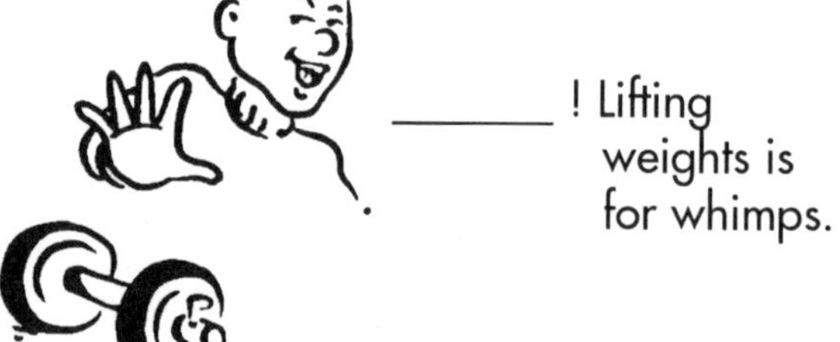

_______ ! Lifting weights is for whimps.

_______ ! Look at that!

Name ______________________________

Crispy Critters

A **conjunction** is a word that is used to join words or groups of words.

Dogs ***and*** *wolves howl.*
I'm happy, ***for*** *today I bought a kitten.*

Write a conjunction in each of the blanks below to complete the Crispy Critters advertisement. Use each conjunction once, but use *and* three times.

Conjunction Bank

neither	nor	either	or	and	not only
but also	while	so	for	yet	

Some cats are treated like pets, ____________ others are treated like family. Show your favorite feline that you love ____________ respect him by bringing home CRISPY CRITTERS kitty food! CRISPY CRITTERS will ____________ make your cat happier, ____________ more energetic and lively. CRISPY CRITTERS comes in four tasty flavors, ____________ choose his favorite. Select ____________ chicken, beef, ____________ seafood. Other cat foods claim to satisfy most cats, ____________ don't back their claims with research. You can be sure that when you buy CRISPY CRITTERS you will ____________ waste money ____________ disappoint your feline friends. CRISPY CRITTERS is delicious ____________ nutritious ____________ a hit every time. Buy CRISPY CRITTERS today, ____________ every day your cat will thank you!

Name ______________________________

Let's Get Together

Contractions tie two words together to make a new word. An apostrophe takes the place of the letters that have been removed.

let + us = let's
that + would = that'd

Write the two small words in each equation that have been put together to make each contraction.

can't = ________ + ________
don't = ________ + ________
isn't = ________ + ________
mustn't = ________ + ________
won't = ________ + ________
shouldn't = ________ + ________
couldn't = ________ + ________
didn't = ________ + ________

aren't = ________ + ________
doesn't = ________ + ________
hasn't = ________ + ________
haven't = ________ + ________
hadn't = ________ + ________
needn't = ________ + ________
weren't = ________ + ________
mightn't = ________ + ________

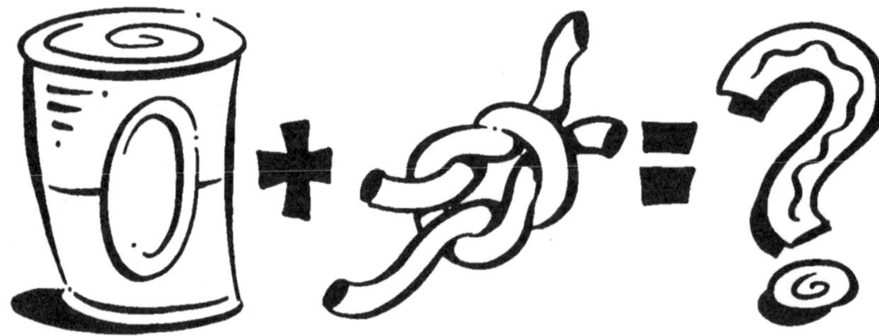

Combine each set of words below to make more contractions.

1. I am ________________
2. he will ________________
3. it is ________________
4. they had ________________
5. could have ________________
6. I had ________________
7. we are ________________
8. we will ________________
9. you are ________________
10. that is ________________
11. she had ________________
12. they have ________________

Name ______________________

At the Front

A **prefix** is one or more syllables added to the beginning of a word to form a new word.

un + believer = unbeliever
mis + trust = mistrust
off + shoot = offshoot

Match a prefix with a root word to form a new word.

_____	1. anti	A. merge
_____	2. tele	B. claim
_____	3. sub	C. call
_____	4. under	D. live
_____	5. pro	E. ordinary
_____	6. en	F. cover
_____	7. re	G. freeze
_____	8. out	H. courage
_____	9. extra	I. meter
_____	10. peri	J. phone

_____	1. post	A. eager
_____	2. bi	B. tanker
_____	3. co	C. organized
_____	4. mini	D. clockwise
_____	5. over	E. cycle
_____	6. extra	F. fine
_____	7. super	G. violent
_____	8. non	H. author
_____	9. ultra	I. skirt
_____	10. counter	J. war

Select words from above and use them to write five sentences.

1. ____
____
2. ____
____
3. ____
____
4. ____
____
5. ____
____

Name ______________________

Bring Up the Rear

A **suffix** is one or more syllables added to the end of a word to form a new word.
love + able = lovable
motion + less = motionless

Complete the classified ads by adding suffixes to the words that are followed by a blank line.

-ing -dom -able -ment -ship -ade -ure -ful -ness -ance

The School Times **Classified** May 2000

Help Wanted

ARE YOU SUFFER_____ from bore_____? You can have a pleasur(e)_____ summer work_____ at the **T h u n d e r C a v e r n s Amuse_____ Park**. For information, call 1-800-FUN-SOAK.

Meetings

Your attend_____ is welcome at the town meet_____ . We will discuss issues of free_____ and citizen_____.

Demand fair_____ and good treat_____ for your pigs. They are pets too! Come and speak about your concerns for our lov(e)_____ swine.

70s Party

WEAR YOUR BELL BOTTOM JEANS and peace-sign jewelry to make a groovy state_____ at this retro bash. The DJ will be play_____ danc(e)_____ music all night long.

For Sale

FRESH AND DELICIOUS lemon_____ and butter cookies with lemon ic(e)_____ made by the varsity cheerleaders.

South City's soccer team is sell_____ chocolate bars. Buy several and enjoy the sweet_____!

Tutoring

DOES ALGEBRA HAVE YOU feel_____ like a fail_____? Sign up for tutor_____. It's help_____ and fun. Call Mr. X for info.

FINISH HIGH SCHOOL and begin your adult life with wis(e)_____! A diploma puts you on the path to a success_____ life.

VOTE! VOTE! VOTE!

Everyone's vote is use_____ in detemin(e)_____ our class officers.
Show your class spirt and ***VOTE TODAY!***

An announce_____ will be made on Monday to congratulate the winners for school govern_____.

BIG MUSIC TRADE

Trade your CDs at the Music King_____ on Saturday at 10:00 A.M. It will be more profit_____ than pain_____. Plus, there will be live entertain_____ and good refresh_____ .

Read_____ the classifieds is good expos(e)_____ to the town's happen_____.

Name ______________________________

The Short of It

Use **abbreviations** with other words or names; never use them by themselves. Avoid using abbreviations in running text. It is more proper to spell out abbreviated words when they appear in a sentence. Capitalize the abbreviations of proper nouns.

I live at 1315 Trail ct., Madison, oh 21461. (incorrect)
My address: 1315 Trail Ct., Madison, OH 21461 (correct)
Christmas is in Dec. (incorrect)
Dec. 25th, 2002 (correct)

Match each noun to its abbreviation.

_____ 1. apartment	_____ 7. Incorporated	A. Rd.	G. pp.
_____ 2. volume	_____ 8. Company	B. cont.	H. vol.
_____ 3. Road	_____ 9. continued	C. Inc.	I. misc.
_____ 4. Reverend	_____ 10. Corporation	D. Corp.	J. lat.
_____ 5. miscellaneous	_____ 11. anonymous	E. Rev.	K. Co.
_____ 6. latitude	_____ 12. pages	F. apt.	L. anon.

In the blanks, write **C** if the abbreviation was used correctly; write **N** if it was not.

_____ 1. We live in an apt.
_____ 2. Apt. 303, Sudsby Rd.
_____ 3. Rev. Martin
_____ 4. My father works for a big corp.
_____ 5. For homework, we were assigned pp. 94–115 in *Great Expectations.*
_____ 6. I hate to watch a show that will be cont. the next day.
_____ 7. Please turn down the vol.
_____ 8. We used money from the misc. category of our budget to buy the gift.
_____ 9. Timber Lumber Co.
_____ 10. Their co. cont. to grow.
_____ 11. Extras and misc.
_____ 12. Our lesson will be cont. tomorrow.

Name ______________________

It's Important!

Capitalize the names of books, movies, plays, songs, poems, television programs, and works of art. Also capitalize the names and titles of people.

Little Women
General Schwartzkopf

Rewrite the following titles using capitals correctly.

Movie:	*a bug's life*	______________
Poem:	"the road not taken"	______________
Play:	*romeo and juliet*	______________
T.V. Show:	"the simpsons"	______________
Art Work:	*the starry night*	______________
Song:	"the star spangled banner"	______________
Book:	*roll of thunder, hear my cry*	______________

Write your favorite titles using capitals correctly.

Movie: ______________________
Poem: ______________________
Play: ______________________
T.V. Show: ______________________
Art Work: ______________________
Song: ______________________
Book: ______________________

Put an **X** on the line if the title is written correctly. If it is not, write the title correctly on the line that follows.

___ the spice Girls ______________________

___ Vice President Gerald R. Ford ______________________

___ *Where In The World Is Carmen San Diego?* ______________________

___ Dr. Sigmund Freud ______________________

___ *how many feet in the bed?* ______________________

___ *the Polar Express* ______________________

Name ______________________

To Whom It May Concern:

Every business letter must have the following:

heading—your name and full address
inside address—the name, title, company, and address of the recipient
date—write out the date in words (e.g., September 14, 1999).
salutation—a formal greeting, "Dear Mr. Buckle,"
body—a concise message written in paragraph form; leave a space between paragraphs.
closing—a formal closing, "Sincerely,"
signature—leave 4 spaces and print your full name; write your signature above it.

Write a business letter to Mr. Fashion, clothing designer of Lookin' Good Fashions Corporation, 500 Style Street, New York City, NY 21112. Suggest your fashion ideas for people your age and request a fashion adjustment that would benefit you personally.

Heading: ______________________________

____

____

Inside Address: ______________________________

____

____

____

Date: ______________________

Salutation: ______________________

Body: ____

____

____

____

____

____

____

____

Closing: ______________________

Signature: ______________________

Full Name: ______________________

Name ______________________________

Louisa May Alcott

A **proper noun** is the name of a particular person, place, or thing. Proper nouns are always capitalized. All other nouns are called **common nouns.** Common nouns are not usually capitalized and refer only to general people, places, or things.

> ***proper nouns**: Joseph, England, Vermont, Pepsi*
> ***common nouns**: boy, country, state, beverage*

Underline all the nouns (both common and proper) in the sentences below.

1. Louisa May Alcott is remembered as a great American author.
2. She was born in Germantown, Pennsylvania, on November 29, 1832.
3. She considered Ralph Waldo Emerson and Henry David Thoreau her friends.
4. Louisa grew up in a poor family in New England where she made and sold dolls' clothes to earn money.
5. When she was a little older, she taught school and began writing.
6. In 1854, Miss Alcott published her first book entitled *Flower Fables.*
7. Several of her stories were published in *Atlantic Monthly.*
8. Eventually, she wrote *Little Women,* a semi-autobiographical novel.
9. Other books based on Alcott's life include *Little Men* and *Jo's Boys.*
10. Today, readers can enjoy her biography, *Invincible Louisa,* written by Cornelia Meigs.

Write the nouns from the sentences in the correct category below.

Common Nouns		Proper Nouns	
______	______	______	______
______	______	______	______
______	______	______	______
______	______	______	______
______	______	______	______
______	______	______	______
______		______	______
		______	______

Name ______________________________

Patches on Jackets and Dresses

Plural nouns represent more than one.

According to the rule given, write the plural form of each of the following words. In each, the first two have been done as examples.

To form the plural of most nouns, just add ***s***. If the noun ends in *s, x, ch, sh, z,* or *ss,* add ***es***.

1. (jacket) *jackets*	5. (dress) *dresses*	9. (patch) ________
2. (shirt) ________	6. (sash) ________	10. (fax) ________
3. (sock) ________	7. (swatch) ________	11. (tie) ________
4. (buzz) ________	8. (belt) ________	12. (jean) ________

For nouns that end in *y* preceded by a vowel, just add ***s***. For nouns that end in *y* preceded by a consonant, change the *y* to *i* and add ***es***.

1. (boy) *boys*	5. (treaty) *treaties*	9. (family) ________
2. (tray) ________	6. (ploy) ________	10. (tragedy) ________
3. (spray) ________	7. (mystery) ________	11. (salary) ________
4. (baby) ________	8. (malady) ________	12. (candy) ________

To form the plural of a word that ends in an *o* preceded by a vowel, add ***s***. For words that end in an *o* preceded by a consonant, usually add ***es***. (There may be some exceptions to this rule.)

1. (tomato) *tomatoes*	5. (zoo) *zoos*	9. (potato) ________
2. (avocado) ________	6. (hero) ________	10. (dingo) ________
3. (buffalo) ________	7. (stereo) ________	11. (kangaroo) ________
4. (zero) ________	8. (rodeo) ________	12. (duo) ________

For words that end in *f* or *fe,* change the *f* to *v* and add ***es***; some of these words simply add ***s***. (You may need to consult a dictionary to be certain.)

1. (scarf) *scarves*	5. (chief) *chiefs*	9. (thief) ________
2. (knife) ________	6. (shelf) ________	10. (half) ________
3. (leaf) ________	7. (elf) ________	11. (belief) ________
4. (motif) ________	8. (life) ________	12. (loaf) ________

Name ______________________________

Concrete or Asphalt?

An **abstract noun** names an idea, quality, or state of mind. It is something not perceivable through any of the five senses.
A **concrete noun** names something that can be seen or touched.

***abstract nouns**: peace, patience, success, sadness*
***concrete nouns**: road, flower, house, animal, Joe*

Circle the concrete nouns. Underline the abstract nouns.

Tony	cement	ambition	idea	land
trust	muscle	precipitation	grace	hope
excitement	talent	sidewalk	honor	faith
New York	sweetness	gravel	influence	hardhat
road	shovel	truck	zero	skyscraper
bucket	power	water	terror	beauty
building	argument	legacy	rock	disgrace
mixer	victory	preference	trowel	love
street	fidelity	asphalt	money	commitment
pride	wood	glue	hate	air
fear	integrity	dog	book	man
music	evil	cooperation	sweat	improvement

Name ______________________

Boy or Girl?

Gender of nouns refers to the sex indicated by the noun. The four genders are
masculine—male
feminine—female
neuter—no sex
indefinite—could be either male or female

***masculine**: knight, prince*
***feminine**: aunt, empress*
***neuter**: chair, car*
***indefinite**: nurse, teacher*

Write the following words under the correct category.

baby	flower	sister	queen	neighbor	rocket
nephew	shoe	husband	principal	mother	uncle
damsel	grandpa	lunch	prince	book	niece
pool	friend	lad	seamstress	princess	teacher
son	table	actor	nurse		

MASCULINE	FEMININE	NEUTER	INDEFINITE
________	________	________	________
________	________	________	________
________	________	________	________
________	________	________	________
________	________	________	________
________	________	________	________
________	________	________	________

Name ____________________

Marching Pride

Nouns that show ownership are called **possessive nouns**. To form the possessive of a singular noun add **'s** . To form a plural possessive add **s'**. If the noun is already in the plural form and ends in an *s*, simply add an apostrophe. If the plural form does not end in an *s*, add **'s** .

singular possessive noun: *Cindy's chair, dog's bone, piano's keys*
plural possessive noun: *ladies' purses, houses' windows, children's lunches, women's club*

Rewrite the phrases by using possessive nouns.

1. Drumsticks belonging to drummers ____________________
2. The reed of the clarinet ____________________
3. Baton belonging to the drum major ____________________
4. Instruments of the musicians ____________________
5. Sound of the tubas ____________________
6. Colorful flags of the color guard ____________________
7. Slide belonging to the trombone ____________________
8. Crash made by cymbals ____________________
9. New uniforms owned by the band ____________________
10. Cases for instruments ____________________
11. Spats for the shoes ____________________
12. Solo of the saxophone ____________________

Add apostrophes to the possessive nouns in the paragraph below.

The bands members march in perfect unison onto the football field. The players hearts beat wildly as the adrenaline pumps throughout their bodies. At the drum majors cue, the musicians lift their instruments. Music and movement explode together in a powerful show for the audiences pleasure. Judges scores are recorded as the band performs. The spectators appreciation is shown with a standing ovation. The bands pride can be felt as they bow before the crowd. At the end of the competition, the bands all stand at attention awaiting the announcement of the final placements and the awarding of their groups trophy.

Name ______________________

All Together!

A **collective noun** names a group of people, places, or things. When a collective noun refers to a group as a unit, it is considered singular. When it refers to the individual members of the group who are acting separately, it is considered plural.

singular collective nouns:

*The **school** of fish live in the cool water.*
*Our **team** usually wins.*

plural collective nouns:

*The **school** of fish are all swimming in different directions to avoid the predator.*
*The **team** are all expected to earn good grades in school.*

Match the collective nouns.

_____	1. colony	A. cotton
_____	2. fleet	B. ships
_____	3. squad	C. lies
_____	4. grove	D. geese
_____	5. bale	E. diamonds
_____	6. gaggle	F. ants
_____	7. pack	G. police
_____	8. nest	H. cards
_____	9. cluster	I. snakes
_____	10. deck	J. trees

Mark the following sentences **S** (singular) or **P** (plural). Circle the correct verb.

_____ 1. The family (is, are) all opening their gifts together.
_____ 2. Grandma's batch of cookies (is, are) baking in the oven.
_____ 3. Mom's set of Christmas china (is, are) waiting on the table.
_____ 4. The cleaning staff (is, are) not working today; they are home with their families.
_____ 5. The company (is, are) due to arrive soon.

Write 4 sentences using the indicated collective nouns. You choose whether to make them singular or plural.

(class) 1. ______________________________
(crowd) 2. ______________________________
(herd) 3. ______________________________
(tribe) 4. ______________________________

predicate nouns

Name ______________________________

Cold-Blooded

> A **predicate noun** is a noun used as a subject complement (the subject of the sentence and the predicate noun represent the same thing). Predicate nouns follow linking verbs.
>
> *Leo was the fiercest lion in the zoo.*
> *Leo = lion*

In each of the following sentences, circle the simple subject and underline the simple predicate noun. Then complete the equation.

1. Reptiles are a specific group of animals. ________________ = ________________
2. They are creatures that are cold-blooded. ________________ = ________________
3. A snake is a reptile. ________________ = ________________
4. The swamp is home to many snakes. ________________ = ________________
5. Iguanas are also members of the reptile family. ________________ = ________________
6. They are lizards that have spines from head to toe. ________________ = ________________
7. The desert is a good habitat for a wide variety of snakes and lizards.

   ________________ = ________________
8. The huge dinosaurs that once roamed the earth were reptiles.

   ________________ = ________________
9. Tyrannosaurus was a flesh-eating dinosaur that lived on land.

   ________________ = ________________
10. Crocodiles and alligators are dangerous reptilian hunters.

    ________________ = ________________
11. The turtle's shell is his home. ________________ = ________________
12. Some people think snakes, lizards, and turtles are good pets.

    ________________ = ________________
13. Frogs are amphibians and do not belong to the reptile family.

    ________________ = ________________
14. Some reptiles are egg layers. ________________ = ________________
15. The python is a constricting snake. ________________ = ________________

Name ______________________________

Dear Santa

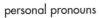

> Pronouns are words that take the place of nouns. A **personal pronoun** indicates the speaker (first person), the one spoken to (second person), or the one spoken about (third person).
>
> ***first-person pronouns***: *I, my, mine, me, we, our, ours, us*
> ***second-person pronouns***: *you, your, yours*
> ***third-person pronouns***: *he, she, it, his, hers, its, him, her, they, their, theirs, them*

In the parentheses next to each personal pronoun, indicate whether the pronoun is first (**1**), second (**2**), or third (**3**) person.

Dear Santa,

I ( ) haven't believed in you ( ) since I ( ) was seven years old, but for many years my ( ) parents shamelessly participated in the scam to deceive me ( ) about your ( ) existence. Year after year they ( ) took me ( ) to see you ( ) at the mall. Tales of your ( ) home in the North Pole and of your ( ) elves further supported their ( ) story. Of course, each Christmas morning I ( ) received several gifts from you ( ). But, the fact is, it ( ) just didn't make sense. How could you ( ) travel around the entire world in just one night, deliver millions of gifts, and eat literally tons of cookies? Impossible, I ( ) say!

This isn't just about me, ( ) either. My ( ) little sister still believes in you, and I ( ) am concerned about her ( ). Is it ( ) good to lie to a little girl? She ( ), like many other trusting children, will one day learn the truth. They ( ) will be heartbroken; their ( ) dreams will be shattered. Santa, how can you ( ) traumatize them ( ) like this? I ( ) urge you ( ) to come clean and tell them ( ) the truth, sir.

Sincerely,
Jeremy

P.S. In case you ( ) are coming to our ( ) house this Christmas Eve, I ( ) could use a new stereo.

Name ______________________________

Colorful Clues

When a pronoun is the subject of the sentence, it is called a **subject pronoun**. When a pronoun is used as the direct object, indirect object, or object of the preposition, it is called an **object pronoun**. A pronoun must agree with its antecedent in both number and gender.

> ***She*** *dropped the book.* (subject)
> *Eric picked* ***it*** *up.* (direct object)
> *Betsy gave* ***him*** *a big smile.* (indirect object)
> *Eric would do anything for* ***her***. (object of the preposition)

Underline the pronoun in each sentence. On the line, write **S** if the pronoun is a subject; write **O** if the pronoun is an object.

_____ 1. Elephants wear it.
_____ 2. It is as dark as the darkest night.
_____ 3. Grandma gave us slippers which perfectly match the delicate hue on the inside of a rabbit's ear.
_____ 4. I bought a chocolate-colored sweater when I was shopping at the mall.
_____ 5. He has eyes that sparkle like beautiful ocean water.
_____ 6. I am the acronym for all of the colors of the rainbow.
_____ 7. The shirt that looks like electric sunshine belongs to him.
_____ 8. Kathryn described to her the cat's fur, which was like fluffy clouds on a sunny day.
_____ 9. We are thinking about painting the exterior of the house the color of pumpkin.
_____ 10. Larry told me that Joe prefers the color of money.
_____ 11. Grapes that had been dipped in nature's royal paint appeared all around him.
_____ 12. Apples, cherries, and some fast cars are dressed in it.

Fill in an appropriate pronoun to take the place of each noun followed by a line. Write the pronoun on the line.

1. Alan and Dutch think the house _______ is the best color of all.
2. I gave my red shoes to Meredith _______.
3. David picked up Lucy _______ in an orange convertible.
4. Laura gave Michael _______ a juicy piece of pink watermelon.
5. Shelby bought a pink teddy bear for her baby sister _______.
6. Renee _______ dropped the pot of hot, red tomato sauce.

Name ____________________

Shoes Galore

> An **antecedent** is the noun to which a pronoun refers. The antecedent may be in the same sentence as the pronoun, or it may appear in another sentence nearby.
>
> *The **guys** shined their shoes after **they** finished walking through the mud.* (*they* refers to *guys*)

Read the paragraph below. Draw an arrow from each italicized pronoun to its antecedent. Then complete the chart below for each pronoun-antecedent pair you found.

My family has a large shoe closet in *our* vestibule. *It* is a mess because everyone just kicks *their* shoes inside. If you would dig through that pile you would find many different kinds of footwear in *it*; my brother's cleats, Mom's three-inch high heels, and Dad's dirty work boots are among *them*. My sister Maggie has about a hundred pair of shoes. *She* has red cowboy boots, summer sandals, weird-looking clogs, and running shoes, just to name a few. *They* are all in the heap. The pile is growing bigger, and *it* is a pain in the neck. Finding a matching pair in that mess takes forever. Someone needs to clean *it* up. I think I'll tell my sister that *she* has to do it!

1. ______________ = ______________
   pronoun antecedent
2. ______________ = ______________
3. ______________ = ______________
4. ______________ = ______________
5. ______________ = ______________
6. ______________ = ______________
7. ______________ = ______________
8. ______________ = ______________
9. ______________ = ______________
10. ______________ = ______________

Name ______________________________

Piranha and Porpoises

A **pronoun** must agree with its antecedent in number and gender.

> ***Madeline*** *is my cousin, and* ***she*** *lives nearby.* (feminine, singular)
> ***Eric and Tim*** *are my cousins, and* ***they*** *live nearby too.* (masculine, plural)
> *Aunt Trudy has a* ***truck****, and* ***it*** *is red.* (neuter, singular)

Circle all of the pronouns in the journal entry below. Write an **F** over all feminine pronouns, an **M** over all masculine pronouns, an **I** over all indefinite pronouns, and an **N** over all neuter pronouns. Also, write an **S** if it is singular or a **P** if it is plural. The first one is done for you.

I–S
(You) won't believe how much fun I've had! Last week my class went to Chicago to visit the Shedd Aquarium. Mrs. Drake split us into six groups, and we all went different directions. My group toured the aquarium cases first. There were all sorts of fish from different parts of the world. The best fish were the South American ones. My friend, Mary, didn't like the piranha. She thought they were creepy. I loved them!

Next we went to see the dolphin show. An aquarium worker came out and stood on rocks in the water. He used whistles and hand signals to make the dolphins jump, swim backwards, and talk. It was really amazing!

Our next stop was in the basement, where we saw the beluga whales. They were the color of snow and played with each other, swimming side by side. We also saw penguins in the basement. Eric and Matt were really mean; they banged on the glass to scare the penguins.

We were allowed only ten minutes in the gift shop, so I only bought a dolphin key chain for my brother. He loves dolphins.

We had a great time, and I can't wait to see it all over again.

Name ___________________________

Sports Fanatics

An **indefinite pronoun** is one that refers generally, not specifically, to people, places, or things. Some indefinite pronouns are always singular, some are always plural, and some may be either singular or plural.

singular indefinite pronouns: *anybody, anyone, another, each, either, everybody, everyone, nobody, no one, neither, one, other, someone, somebody, everything, anything, something*

plural indefinite pronouns: *many, both, few, several, others*

singular or plural indefinite pronouns: *all, any, most, some, none*

In each of the following sentences, underline the indefinite pronouns. Circle the verb that agrees in number with the indefinite pronoun acting as the subject.

1. Everyone in my family (love, loves) to watch football on Sunday afternoons.
2. Several of my friends and I (play, plays) baseball.
3. After school, some of the guys (practice, practices) basketball on our street.
4. In our little town, no one (know, knows) much about ice hockey.
5. Many (choose, chooses) tennis while others (prefer, prefers) racquetball.
6. All of the schools in our community (has, have) soccer teams.
7. Does anyone (consider, considers) pool a sport?
8. Someone in our class (claim, claims) table tennis is an Olympic sport.
9. In the ring, both boxers (take, takes) a beating.
10. Each speed skater (race, races) against the clock to get the best time possible.
11. Fortunately, somebody (was able, were able) to get us tickets to the ice-skating competition.
12. Either of them could (participate, participates) in the track and field finals.
13. Few of my friends (dive, dives) well.
14. I think everything about sumo wrestling (is, are) totally cool.
15. Nobody (call, calls) chess a sport. Right?

Name ______________________________

Peanuts

A **possessive pronoun** is one which indicates ownership or possession. Possessive pronouns include: **my**, **mine**, **your**, **yours**, **his**, **her**, **hers**, **its**, **our**, **ours**, **their**, **theirs**.

*He forgot **his** peanuts as he raced out of school.*

Read the story, underline all of the pronouns, and circle all of the possessive pronouns.

Lou loved peanuts. Lou's mom bought huge amounts of peanuts to keep him satisfied. But, despite her attempts, her son's ravenous appetite for peanuts grew with each passing day. Lou carried them in his pockets, which bulged like satchels at his waist. Everywhere we went he shucked his peanuts, leaving a crunchy trail of shells behind him. The problem increased until our gym teacher finally refused to let him play volleyball after all the players began slipping on his shellings. Our teammates lost their patience, too, and suggested Lou sit out. He protested, but our team just yelled, "You're through, Lou!"

Then, on Saturday, Lou met his terrible fate. While enjoying a riveting performance at the circus and munching feverishly on his favorite snack, my friend Lou was attacked by a hungry baby elephant. She apparently broke free when she smelled Lou's pocketful of peanuts. She thought the peanuts should be hers. And so, Lou's peanut-eating days are at an end. It pains me to report the conclusion of this tale about a dear friend of mine.

Poor Lou, we will miss you.

Name ________________________

Who? What?

An **interrogative pronoun** introduces a question. Interrogative pronouns include: **who**, **whom**, **whose**, **what**, and **which**.

> ***Who*** *is at the door?*
> ***What*** *does he want?*

Underline the interrogative pronouns in the sentences below.

A Good Movie

1. With whom did you see the movie?
2. Whose ticket stub is this?
3. What did you think of the special effects?
4. Which actor was your favorite?
5. Who do you think would enjoy seeing this film?

Using the interrogative pronouns below, write five sentences that belong under each title.

The Big Game

1. Who ________________________
2. Whom ________________________
3. Whose ________________________
4. What ________________________
5. Which ________________________

An Effective Punishment

1. Who ________________________
2. Whom ________________________
3. Whose ________________________
4. What ________________________
5. Which ________________________

Name ____________________

Pearls

> **Relative pronouns** are used to introduce groups of words that modify nouns. **Interrogative pronouns** introduce a question.
>
> ***relative pronouns****: who, whose, which, that*
> *People* ***who*** *read a lot are often very intelligent.*
>
> ***interrogative pronouns****: who, whom, whose, what, which*
> ***Whose*** *book is this?*

Circle the relative pronouns in the paragraph.

The book that I read for my report really made me think. *The Pearl*, which was written by John Steinbeck, is a parable about survival and overcoming oppression. I am one who has faced little prejudice in my life, yet there are many other people who struggle their entire lives to break free of injustice. These men and women, whose lives exemplify the test of perseverance, inspire me. I appreciate the story that Steinbeck told, which demonstrates very well the power of oppression and the importance of perseverance.

Underline all the relative and interrogative pronouns in the sentences below. Write an **I** if it is interrogative or an **R** if it is relative.

_____ 1. Whose pearl necklace is this?
_____ 2. She wore pearls that were creamy white.
_____ 3. My mom, who is a pearl lover, owns many beautiful pieces of pearl jewelry.
_____ 4. A perfect pearl, which is formed in an oyster, can be extremely valuable.
_____ 5. Which color pearl do you prefer?
_____ 6. Hey, to whom does this pearl necklace belong?
_____ 7. I prefer black pearls, which are beautiful and unusual.
_____ 8. Pearls that are cultivated naturally are rare.
_____ 9. Who wants to dive for pearls?
_____ 10. What makes a pearl valuable?

Name ______________________________

G-nip, G-nop

Reflexive pronouns are formed by adding ***self*** or ***selves*** to certain forms of personal pronouns. They reflect the action of the verb back to the subject. **Intensive pronouns** are formed in the same way, but they give intensity back to the noun or pronoun just named.

> ***reflexive***: *I taught* ***myself*** *to play table tennis.*
> ***intensive***: *The table* ***itself*** *comes from the sporting shop down the street.*

Underline the reflexive and intensive pronouns in the sentences below. Write an **R** if it is a reflexive pronoun; write an **I** if it is intensive.

_____ 1. We all taught ourselves to play table tennis.
_____ 2. The table itself stands in our basement.
_____ 3. Dad himself carried it downstairs on Andrew's eleventh birthday.
_____ 4. I myself couldn't wait to grab a paddle and start playing.
_____ 5. The boys immediately placed themselves around the game table.
_____ 6. Christina proclaimed herself to be a pro.
_____ 7. You are probably asking yourself who actually played the first game.
_____ 8. It was Mom herself who made the first challenge.
_____ 9. My father himself quickly accepted it, and they began to play.
_____ 10. They played themselves into an intensely competitive sweat.
_____ 11. We took turns teaching ourselves to volley the ball back and forth.
_____ 12. I myself like the game so much that I can play for hours each day.

Write two sentences that include reflexive pronouns and two sentences that include intensive pronouns.

(reflexive) 1. ______________________________
(reflexive) 2. ______________________________

(intensive) 1. ______________________________
(intensive) 2. ______________________________

Name ______________________________

The Case of the Missing Cow

> The use of **who** and **whom** is determined by the pronoun's function in the clause. Generally, **who** is used as the subject of a sentence or a clause. **Whom** is used as the object (direct, indirect, or object of the preposition).
>
> *With **whom** did you see the cow last night?*
> ***Who** is a suspect?*

Read the sentences below and circle the correct pronoun.

1. Farmer Frank is the one (who, whom) owns the cow.
2. Steve Grant is the officer in (who, whom) Farmer Frank has placed his trust to find her.
3. Do you know (who, whom) has taken Farmer Frank's cow, Bessie?
4. Farmer Frank's wife, (who, whom) gave the cow as a gift, has been crying since Bessie's disappearance.
5. (Who, Whom) would want a huge plastic cow anyway?
6. The police at the station to (who, whom) she spoke have tried to calm her down.
7. There is a rumor that someone (who, whom) is planning a harmless prank has taken the plastic bovine.
8. To (who, whom) was this information given?
9. Mrs. McGrady is the one (who, whom) heard that the cow might show up on the high school roof.
10. She did not know (who, whom) might be instigating such a stunt.
11. The students (who, whom) attend Dairyville High are being questioned.
12. No one seems to know anything about those (who, whom) are involved.
13. Farmer Frank released a statement saying that he was not angry with the pranksters (who, whom) have borrowed his cow, but he is asking that they return her unharmed.
14. Officer Grant is the one with (who, whom) you should speak if you have any information about Bessie the missing cow.

Using **who** and **whom**, write a paragraph explaining the solution to the case of the missing cow.

____

____

____

____

____

____

Name ______________________

Little Boy Blue

A **verb** is a word that expresses action or a state of being.
action: go, jump, breathe, love, break
state of being: is, are, look, seem

__action__: Little Boy Blue __deserted__ his toys.
__state of being__: The little boy __is__ blue.

Underline the verbs in this poem written by Eugene Field. Mark them **A** (action) or **S** (state of being).

Little Boy Blue

The little toy dog is covered with dust,
But sturdy and staunch he stands;
And the little toy soldier is red with rust,
And his musket molds in his hands.
Time was when the little toy dog was new,
And the soldier was passing fair;
And that was the time when our Little Boy Blue
Kissed them and put them there.

"Now, don't you go till I come," he said,
"And don't you make any noise!"
So, toddling off to his trundle-bed,
He dreamed of the pretty toys;
And, as he was dreaming, an angel song
Awakened our Little Boy Blue–
Oh! the years are many, the years are long,
But the little toy friends are true!

Aye, faithful to Little Boy Blue they stand,
Each in the same old place—
Awaiting the touch of a little hand,
The smile of a little face;
And they wonder, as waiting the long years through
In the dust of that little chair,
What has become of our Little Boy Blue,
Since he kissed them and put them there.

—Eugene Field (1850–1895)

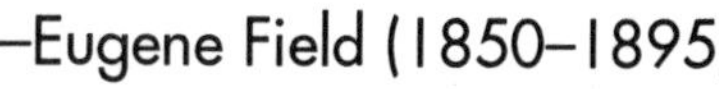

Name ______________________________

Dazzling Stars

A **verb** is a word that expresses action or a state of being.
action: *cry, leap, laugh, win, peel*
state of being: *looks, is, are, were, seems*

Circle all of the verbs in the poster below. Then, write the verbs under the appropriate category.

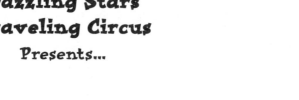

Dazzling Stars
Traveling Circus
Presents...

- Crazy, unicycle-riding clowns are experts who make children smile.
- Trapeze artists fly through the air performing awesome stunts.
- Jumbo elephants demonstrate strength and grace.
- The bearded lady will fascinate and intrigue.
- The lion tamer risks life and limb.
- Curly poodles are dressed in frills and dance for everyone's enjoyment.
- The thousand-pound man is a sight to behold.
- Elegant horses seem royal as they prance and bow with pride.
- Daredevil Dave shoots himself out of a cannon with terrifying speed.
- Talented tumblers look beautiful in glittery costumes and amaze young and old alike.
- The knife thrower displays his skill and bravery as he flings sharpened blades.

Action Verbs

1. ______________
2. ______________
3. ______________
4. ______________
5. ______________
6. ______________
7. ______________
8. ______________
9. ______________
10. ______________
11. ______________
12. ______________
13. ______________
14. ______________
15. ______________
16. ______________

State of Being Verbs

1. ______________
2. ______________
3. ______________
4. ______________
5. ______________

subject–verb agreement

Name ______________________________

Volcanoes

A **verb** must agree with its **subject** in number. A singular subject requires a singular verb, and a plural subject requires a plural verb. **Note:** The number of a subject is not changed by a phrase or a clause that might follow it.

singular: *The volcano erupts.* *The volcano, which has looked threatening for hours, erupts.*

plural: *The volcanoes erupt.* *The volcanoes that line the mountaintop erupt.*

In the following sentences, circle the correct verb.

1. Volcanic eruptions (occur, occurs) when magma (rise, rises) through the earth's crust and emerges onto the surface.
2. Magma that (erupt, erupts) onto the earth's surface (is, are) called lava.
3. Just about all types of lava (contain, contains) silicon and oxygen.
4. When lava flows over the earth, the land that lies in its path (is destroyed, are destroyed).
5. Most Hawaiian eruptions (is, are) gentle.
6. Some others (blast, blasts) huge amounts of volcanic ash high into the air.
7. After a powerful blast, volcanic ash (settle, settles) everywhere.
8. Volcanic islands (emerge, emerges) from the ocean when ash and lava (build, builds) up over years.
9. Legend (say, says) that when Pele the volcano goddess becomes angry, she causes volcanoes to erupt.

Write subjects that agree with the following verbs.

______________ swing	______________ stay	______________ have
______________ eats	______________ tell	______________ is
______________ shows	______________ are	______________ cares

Write verbs that agree with the following subjects.

restaurants ______________	pirates ______________	car ______________
ladders ______________	children ______________	videos ______________
frog ______________	snow ______________	facts ______________

Name ____________________

Chocolate

The **tense** of a verb indicates the time in which an action takes place.

Present tense indicates action or being that is happening now.

*I **eat** chocolate kisses.*

Past tense indicates action or being that was completed in the past.

*I **ate** chocolate kisses.*

Future tense indicates action or being that will take place in the future. The auxiliary verb *will* is usually used with the principal verb to form the future tense.

*I **will eat** chocolate kisses.*

Underline the verb in each sentence. Identify the tense of each verb by marking **P** (present tense), **PA** (past tense), or **F** (future tense).

_____ 1. I will always love every kind of chocolate.

_____ 2. Delicious chocolate comes from bumpy green pods on tropical trees in Central and South America.

_____ 3. Chocolate beans were as valuable to the Aztecs as money.

_____ 4. The trees were called *kakahuatl* (ca-ca-hoo-AH-tul) by the Aztecs.

_____ 5. Today the kakahuatl tree is called the cacao (cah-cow) tree.

_____ 6. Only rich Aztecs drank chocolatl (show-co-lah-tul).

_____ 7. Cacao trees are grown in tropical countries around the world.

_____ 8. Cacao trees have long, shiny, bright green leaves with bunches of little flowers on their football-shaped pods.

_____ 9. A cacao pod contains 20–40 semi-purple beans.

_____ 10. The cacao beans are bitter.

_____ 11. Then they will be dried in the sun.

_____ 12. These special beans will eventually become chocolate liquor.

Name ____________________

Origami Bird

An **infinitive** is a present tense verb preceded by the word *to* (to + verb). An infinitive can act as a noun, an adjective, or an adverb.

George sat on the front step ***to finish*** *his paper bird.*

Underline all of the infinitives in the directions for creating an origami bird.

1. It is easy to create an origami bird, but you must be careful to follow the directions exactly.

1\.
2\.

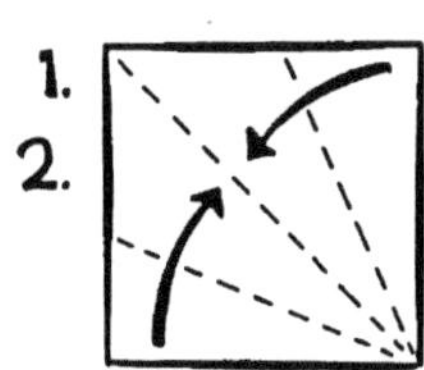

2. To begin, you must cut out a perfect square (6" or about 15 cm is good) of paper. Then fold the outer edges to the middle on the dotted lines as shown.
3. Now your paper should resemble a kite. Fold the "kite" in half in order to touch the top corner to the bottom corner.
4. Fold the tip down to form a beak.
5. To continue, fold your paper back, as shown, on the dotted lines.

3\.

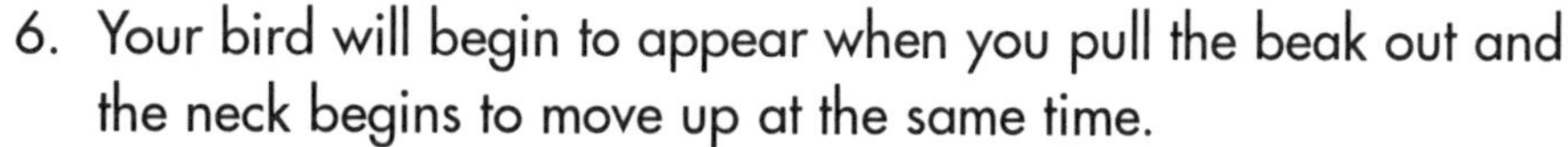

6. Your bird will begin to appear when you pull the beak out and the neck begins to move up at the same time.
7. Press the paper firmly at the stars to make the neck stay in place.

8. It is important to fold the bottom points up on each side to add feet to your creation.

4\.

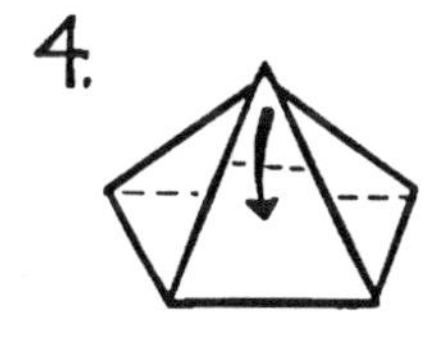

9. Try again by using different colors and sizes of paper to design dozens of origami birds.

5\.

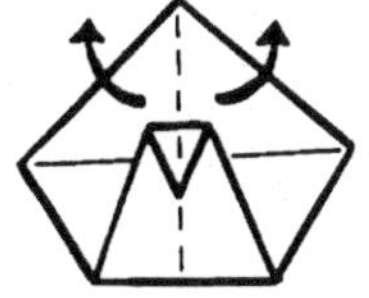

6\.

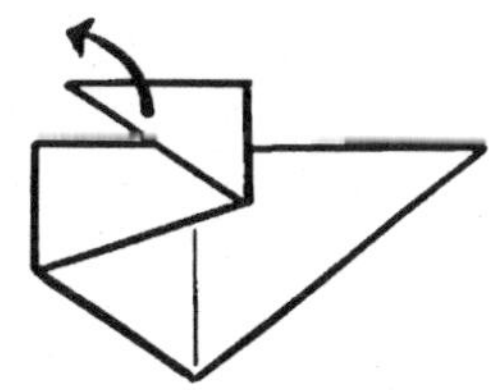

7\.

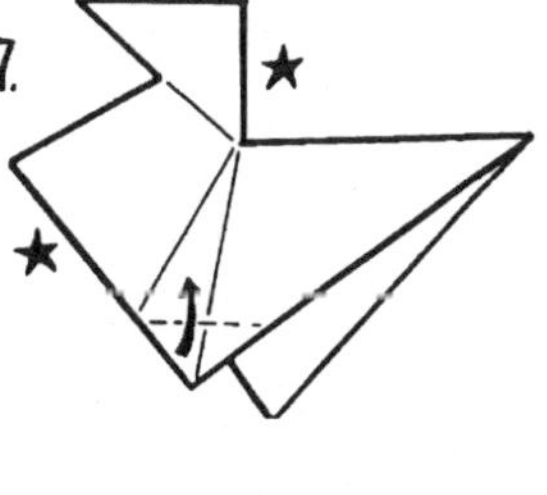

8\.

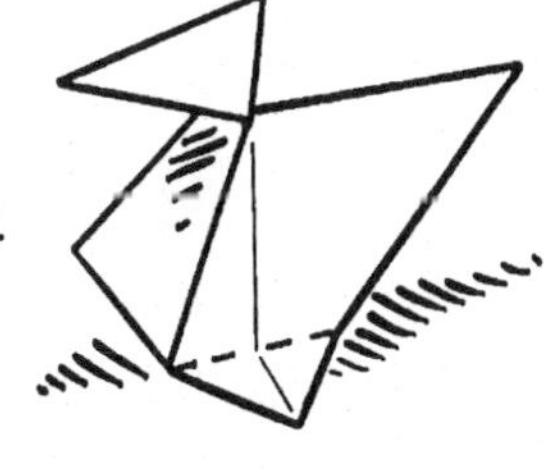

Name ____________________________

Cooking Up a Storm

> An **infinitive** is a present tense verb usually preceded by *to*. It is often used as a noun serving as a subject or a predicate noun. An infinitive phrase includes modifiers, a complement, or a subject, which act together as a single part of speech.
>
> ***subject***: ***To make dinner*** *for Grandma was Lesley's reason for taking a cooking class.*
>
> ***predicate noun***: *Lesley's hope is* ***to make a seven-course meal.***

Underline the infinitives or infinitive phrases in each of the following sentences.

1. To cook is my grandma's favorite hobby.
2. She likes to shop for interesting ingredients.
3. I was hoping to visit her after school.
4. One of my goals is to learn to make meatballs like Grandma's.
5. To make spaghetti is Grandma Elsie's specialty.
6. Her favorite kitchen experience is to create chocolate-covered cream puffs.
7. According to my grandma, the key to becoming a good cook is to practice.
8. To watch my grandma in the kitchen is very entertaining.
9. She always seems to make a big mess before her masterpieces are done.
10. To clean up the kitchen is not fun unless you are cleaning with Grandma.
11. Her quick clean-up method is to put everything in the dishwasher so that we can sit down and eat something delicious.
12. I like to cook and eat with Grandma Elsie.

In each of the following sentences, underline the infinitive phrase used as a noun and indicate if it is a subject (**S**) or a predicate noun (**PN**).

_____ 1. To give a great party was Candy's plan.

_____ 2. To write the guest list was her first priority.

_____ 3. Her next step was to plan the menu and decorations.

_____ 4. Her idea was to celebrate with a Hawaiian theme.

_____ 5. To offer her guests grass skirts and leis seemed like a good idea.

_____ 6. To hula dance would also be a fun activity.

_____ 7. To view her work hours later gave her pleasure.

_____ 8. All that was left was to enjoy the party.

Name ______________________________

Riddle Me This

The mood of the verb indicates the attitude or viewpoint behind the verb's expression. The **imperative mood** indicates a command or a request. The subject is always *you*, though this is not always expressed.

Please, wake me up at 7:00.
Make up your mind.

Write **Y** in the space if the sentence uses the imperative mood. Write **N** if it does not.

_____ 1. Mow the lawn.

_____ 2. Quiet down, please.

_____ 3. She dances gracefully.

_____ 4. The pizza is hot.

_____ 5. Go outside to play.

_____ 6. The flowers smell nice.

_____ 7. Wait for me!

_____ 8. Mustard tastes gross.

_____ 9. Just behave yourself.

_____ 10. Please pass the salt.

_____ 11. He's coming home now.

_____ 12. Take the garbage out.

For each riddle below, write your own answer using the imperative mood. Remember to write a command or a request.

1. What did the tired light say?

____

2. What did the whistling teapot say?

____

3. What did the chicken's mother say before he crossed the road?

____

4. What did the flowers say to the lady shopping at the greenhouse?

____

5. What did Santa say to the elves?

____

6. What kind of assignment is given to the people who go to the mall?

____

Name ______________________________

"Eggs"tremely Active

A verb is in the **active voice** when the subject of the sentence is performing the action.

*The bird **laid** an egg.*
*A large speckled egg **hatched**.*

In the following paragraph, underline each simple subject and circle each active voice verb.

Hen's eggs take just twenty-one days to hatch. The hen must sit on her eggs to keep them warm until the chicks are born. Inside the egg, yolk and white provide nourishment for the bird. A red spot on the yolk will turn into a chick after three weeks. Tiny organs such as a beak and a stomach form. The wings and feet develop too. Sticky feathers cover the chick, and the chick's egg tooth forms. Tiny holes in the egg's shell allow air to pass in and out. The chick's head lies near an air pocket at one end of the egg. The chick pushes its beak into the pocket to get its first breath of air. The chick uses its sharp egg tooth to break out of its shell. Finally, the baby bird dries and fluffs its yellow feathers and begins its search for food.

Read the numbered sentences below and underline the active voice verbs.

1. As an adult, a chicken's weight ranges from about 1.1 pounds (.5 kg) to more than 11 pounds (5 kg).
2. Feathers, which cover most of the body, will keep the chicken warm in cold weather.
3. A chicken's feathers also come in a range of colors and patterns.
4. Unlike some other birds, chickens develop fleshy structures called the comb and wattle.
5. These structures keep the chicken cool and help in recognition.
6. The shape and size of the comb vary from breed to breed.

Name ______________________

Around the World with Sweets

When the subject is receiving the action, a **passive voice** verb is being used.

The sweet treats ***were enjoyed*** *by everyone.*

In the following sentences, underline the passive voice verbs. Then, rewrite each sentence using the active voice.

1. Tamarind (tam-uh-rund) is a brown, sticky treat from the tamarind pod, which is eaten by children in India.

   ____

   ____

2. Tamarillos (tam-uh-RILL-oze) are tangy, red or yellow, football-shaped fruits, which are enjoyed by New Zealanders.

   ____

   ____

3. In the Caribbean, a sweet treat called sugar cane is enjoyed by many.

   ____

   ____

4. In South America, green, heart-shaped cherimoyas (chair-ee-MOY-yuz) are favored by the children of Chile.

   ____

   ____

5. A sweet and crunchy, brown root, called jicama (hee-kuh-mah), is served by the people of Mexico.

   ____

   ____

6. The breadfruit, a tropical fruit that tastes like baked bread, has been made a favorite by natives of the Pacific Islands.

   ____

   ____

   ____

7. Pomegranates, round fruits with red, leathery rinds, have been cultivated throughout the Mediterranean world for a very long time.

   ____

   ____

   ____

Name ______________________

The Scavenger Hunt

A verb is in the **active voice** when the subject performs the action. A verb is in the **passive voice** when the subject receives the action. (Passive voice should be used sparingly. Active voice expresses action in a natural, more direct way.)

***active voice**: We played the scavenger hunt game at school.*
***passive voice**: The scavenger hunt game was played by us at school.*

Identify the verbs in the following sentences by labeling them **A** (active) or **P** (passive). If the verb is in passive voice, rewrite the sentence, changing the verb to active voice.

_____ 1. The scavenger hunt game was played by the entire class.

____

____

_____ 2. The class was divided into two teams by Mr. Mack, our homeroom teacher.

____

____

_____ 3. We called our team "The Scavengers."

____

_____ 4. The other team gave themselves the name "The Search Party."

____

____

_____ 5. All of the clues were carefully hidden by our teacher.

____

____

_____ 6. At the beginning of the game, each team was given the first clue by Mr. Mack.

____

____

_____ 7. We found it hidden by the drinking fountain next to the principal's office.

____

____

_____ 8. After a long and challenging hunt for clues, the game was finally won by "The Search Party."

____

____

Name ______________________________

No-Bake Cookies

A **regular verb** is one which forms its past tense and past participle by adding ***d*** or ***ed*** to the present tense verb form. An **irregular verb** is any verb which does not form its past and past participle by adding ***d*** or ***ed*** to its present tense.

	present	***past***	***past participle***
regular	*bake*	*baked*	*(have, has, had) baked*
irregular	*eat*	*ate*	*(have, has, had) eaten*

In the recipe below, circle the verbs. Then, write each verb and its forms in the proper column below.

Combine 2 cups (480 ml) sugar, 1/2 cup (120 ml) milk, 1/2 cup (120 ml) butter, 1/2 cup (120 ml) cocoa in a 2-quart (1.9 l) saucepan. Place the pan on the burner at medium heat. Stir constantly. Bring to a boil; boil for one minute. Remove from heat and add 1/2 cup (120 ml) smooth peanut butter, 2 teaspoons (10 ml) vanilla, and 3 cups (720 ml) dry oatmeal. Mix ingredients together well. Tear a large piece of wax paper from the roll and lay it on the counter top away from the heat. On the wax paper, drop spoonfuls of the mixture. Chill the cookies in the refrigerator for quick results.

Regular Verbs

present | past | past participle

1. ______________________________
2. ______________________________
3. ______________________________
4. ______________________________
5. ______________________________
6. ______________________________
7. ______________________________
8. ______________________________
9. ______________________________

Irregular Verbs

present | past | past participle

1. ______________________________
2. ______________________________
3. ______________________________
4. ______________________________

Name ______________________

So Weird!

An **irregular verb** is any verb that does not follow the *d* or *ed* pattern for forming its past and past participle.

	present	***past***	***past participle***
regular verb	*jump*	*jumped*	*(have, has, had) jumped*
irregular verb	*go*	*went*	*(have, has, had) gone*

For each of the irregular verbs below, write the missing forms. You may need to refer to your grammar text for help with some of the answers.

Present	Past	Past Participle (have, has, or had)
think	thought	
spend		spent
	drove	driven
begin	began	
eat		eaten
fall	fell	
	hid	hidden
write		
	spoke	
hear		
		torn
	took	
weave		
	stole	
		chosen

Write a sentence for each tense of the irregular verb *fly*.

(present) 1. ______________________________

____

(past) 2. ______________________________

____

(past participle) 3. ______________________________

____

Name ___________________________

Anna Advice

A **verb phrase** is a group of words that does the work of a single verb. The phrase includes one principal verb and one or more helping verbs (usually forms of *to be*).

Anna Advice ***has been giving*** *good advice for years.*

In the letter below, underline all of the verb phrases and circle the helping verbs.

Dear Anna Advice,

I have been trying to make a difficult decision, and I am hoping you can help me out. All of my friends are planning to go skiing next weekend, and they want me to go along too. The problem is that I have been skiing before and have hated it. I was totally terrified by the ski lift (I guess I was afraid of heights or something), and I was freaked out when I literally flew down the hill completely out of control. I had vowed I would never go skiing again, but now I am feeling like a baby and am wondering what I should do. Please help.

Sincerely,
Afraid to Swoosh in Pennsylvania

Dear Afraid to Swoosh,

I have been considering your dilemma carefully and have finally concluded that you should be honest with your friends. I would bet that they will understand how you are feeling. Certainly you could join them on the skiing trip but skip the skiing. Who knows, maybe another one of your friends is having the same concern! I am sure you will have a great time!

Sincerely,
Anna Advice

Name ______________________________

Giant Pandas

A **linking verb** does not show action. It connects the subject of the sentence to a word or words in the predicate. Forms of the word *to be* are the most common linking verbs, but other words can serve to join the ideas in a sentence as well. Any verb that can be substituted by a form of *to be* is a linking verb.

Pandas ***are*** *enormous animals.*

Ming Ling ***felt*** *soft.*

In each of the following sentences, underline the linking verb and circle the words in the subject and the predicate that are joined (or connected) by it.

1. Giant pandas seem friendly and harmless.
2. They are very beautiful and look like cuddly teddy bears.
3. The giant panda is a native of the dense bamboo forests of China.
4. The Chinese people are extremely proud of pandas and have made them a symbol of their country.
5. Bamboo is the panda's primary food; it makes up almost 99 percent of the bear's diet.
6. Thousands of years ago, bamboo forests were bountiful in eastern China, and giant pandas dwelled there.
7. The biggest panda ever weighed was almost 400 pounds (182 kg), but the average panda weighs over 200 pounds (91 kg).
8. Panda cubs can be very small, weighing only about 5 ounces (140 g).
9. The bones of a panda are large, thick, and very heavy.
10. Pandas seem very happy in their lush, green habitat.
11. Pandas in the zoo are a pleasure to watch.
12. Unfortunately, giant pandas are among the most endangered animals on the earth today.

Name ____________________

Greeny

A **linking verb** does not show action. It connects the subject of the sentence to a word or words in the predicate. Commonly used linking verbs are forms of *to be*. Other linking verbs include *grow, become, appear, taste*, and *remain*. If you can substitute a form of *to be* for a verb, it is probably a linking verb.

*The plant **was** tall.*
*The plant **appeared** tall.*

Underline the linking verb in each sentence and circle the word or words that it links.

Greeny

Greeny, the bean plant, appeared as a bud.
He remained rather small and was labeled a dud.
The warm rains then fell 'till the sun appeared bright.
Greeny the bean plant said, "I'll be all right!
Watch me become big, straight, and tall.
I no longer look little, but biggest of all."
Soon he was proud to lie on a plate.
And, the diners agreed, "He tastes perfectly great!"

Write sentences about vegetables using the following linking verbs.

1. (look) ____________________
2. (become) ____________________
3. (appear) ____________________
4. (taste) ____________________
5. (remain) ____________________

Name ______________________

Mighty Minerals

A **subject complement** is a word that comes after a linking verb and refers back to the subject. Subject complements can be nouns, pronouns, or adjectives. A noun used as a subject complement is called a **predicate noun.** When a pronoun is used, it is called a **predicate pronoun**. An adjective used as a subject complement is called a **predicate adjective**.

***predicate noun**:* *The ruby is a **gem**.*
***predicate pronoun**:* *The ruby is **it**.*
***predicate adjective**:* *The ruby is **red**.*

In the following sentences, circle all of the subject complements. Then, draw an arrow from the subject complement to the subject and underline the linking verb. On the line, write **PN** for predicate noun, **PPN** for predicate pronoun, and **PA** for predicate adjective.

_____ 1. A person who studies minerals is a mineralogist.

_____ 2. Minerals are useful.

_____ 3. Minerals that make metals are ore minerals.

_____ 4. All minerals are uniquely beautiful.

_____ 5. Emeralds are green.

_____ 6. One very strong mineral is the diamond.

_____ 7. If you're looking for a very hard mineral, the diamond is it.

_____ 8. No mineral is harder.

_____ 9. Graphite, however, is very soft.

_____ 10. The black substance in a pencil that leaves a mark on paper is it.

_____ 11. One property of minerals is specific gravity.

_____ 12. Having a very high specific gravity, gold ore is extremely heavy.

_____ 13. The hobby of mineral collecting is popular.

_____ 14. Occasionally, obtaining certain minerals is a challenge.

_____ 15. Minerals are the most common solid materials on earth.

Name ______________________

For the Love of Insects

A **transitive verb** is an action verb that is followed by a direct object. The verb "transmits" the action from the subject to the object. The direct object can be found by asking *what* or *whom* after the verb.

Insects (S) ***fill*** *our world* (DO)*.*

Many insects (S) ***help*** *man* (DO)*, but some insects* (S) ***destroy*** *gardens* (DO)*.*

In each of the sentences in the paragraph, underline the transitive verbs and label the direct objects with a **DO**.

Most insects eat plants. Some feed on roots or decaying plant life. The majority of insects favor stems and leaves, but some species devour other insects. Dragonflies catch mosquitos, midges, and small moths. Some giant waterbugs catch fish twice their own size. A praying mantis will "pray" motionless for hours before snaring an insect. The helpful ladybug eliminates pesky aphids each time it dines.

People dislike insects for various reasons, however. Destructive insects annihilate crops, and others carry terrible diseases. Often people spray poisonous insecticides to control the troublemakers. Unfortunately, insecticides harm helpful insects as well. Today, scientists seek better solutions to our insect problems while they rely on the many useful insects to help them out.

In the numbered sentences below, underline the direct object and draw a line from the transitive verb to the direct object.

1. Scientists have discovered about one million species of insects.
2. Insects pollinate many of our crops and provide us with honey and other products.
3. Like humans, insects build bridges, apartment buildings, and homes.
4. They also raise crops and keep "livestock."
5. Scientists estimate the average number of insects per square mile of land equals the number of people on earth!
6. The insect world encompasses some of the most attractive and fascinating animals on earth.

Name ______________________

Morning Munchies

An **intransitive verb** does not need a direct object to complete its meaning. It does not direct action toward an object or a person. An intransitive verb is frequently followed by a prepositional phrase.

S PP
*The cereal **was eaten** in the morning.*

In the sentences on the cereal box below, underline the intransitive verbs and circle the subjects. Write the intransitive verbs you find on the lines to the right.

Morning Munchies

Finally, a cereal for the morning munchies has arrived! When toast or frozen waffles won't cut it, *Morning Munchies* will. Inside each box, the flavor waits. The crunch of sweetened nuts, along with the chew of dried fruits satisfies everytime. Even covered with milk, this breakfast sensation crunches. Other breakfast cereals fear for their future, but *Morning Munchies* worries about nothing. Although the popularity of other cereals may fade away, *Morning Munchies* will remain. Great-tasting and super-crunchy *Morning Munchies* works for everyone. So, when your hunger strikes, fill up on *Morning Munchies.*

____
____
____
____
____
____
____
____
____
____

Name ______________________________

Gone Fishin'

A **transitive verb** is an action verb that is followed by a direct object. The verb "transmits" the action from the subject to the object. An **intransitive verb** does not need an object to complete its meaning. It is frequently followed by a prepositional phrase.

***transitive**: We **caught** a fish.*
***intransitive**: I **fish** with my dad.*

In the spaces below, write **T** if the sentence contains a transitive verb; write **IT** if it contains an intransitive verb. Then, underline the subject and the object (if one is present).

_____ 1. Live bait wiggles in the covered container.

_____ 2. I am wearing my new fishing hat.

_____ 3. Dad stocked the tackle box with all of our gear.

_____ 4. We packed a sack lunch of sandwiches and apples.

_____ 5. I prefer fishing in the boat.

_____ 6. Dad usually fishes from the pier.

_____ 7. We catch perch and catfish.

_____ 8. Our catch is placed in a wire mesh basket.

_____ 9. The sun shines brightly in the sky.

_____ 10. I will probably get a sunburn today.

_____ 11. I really don't mind baiting my own hook.

_____ 12. Dad smiles at me.

_____ 13. Before we head home, I want to catch a super-big fish.

_____ 14. Dad throws back a big, ugly dogfish.

_____ 15. We will definitely brag about our fishing conquests.

_____ 16. My dad likes fishing with a girl like me.

Name ______________________________

Duke's Dilemma

Lie means to recline, to rest, or to remain in a reclining position. The principal parts of *lie* are *lie, lay, (have, has, had) lain.* **Lay** means to put something down or to place something somewhere. Its principal parts are *lay, laid, (have, has, had) laid.* This verb always has an object.

lie: *His pets **lie** on the carpet waiting for him to arrive.*

lay: *When he arrives, he **lays** a treat for each of them on the floor.*

Circle the correct verb in each of the following sentences.

1. Fiffi often (lays, lies) on the cushion in the bay window, letting the sun's rays warm her.
2. Her toy mouse is (laying, lying) nearby.
3. She meows happily when Mrs. McGregor (lays, lies) a bowl of milk in the corner.
4. She (lays, lies) a kitty snack near the bowl, too.
5. While the cat enjoys the treat, Duke, the dog, (lays, lies) lazily on his rug in front of the fireplace.
6. Fiffi has never (laid, lain) in Duke's chosen spot.
7. Once, when Mrs. McGregor had (lain, laid) Duke's favorite rug in a different spot, the dog whimpered and growled for hours.
8. Fiffi was so nervous, she could not (lay, lie) comfortably anywhere.
9. Fiffi (lay, laid) in the windowsill meowing unhappily.
10. As soon as Mr. McGregor came home, he removed his shoes and (lay, laid) his hat on the table.
11. He noticed immediately that Duke was not (laying, lying) in his usual spot.
12. Mr. McGregor promptly (lay, laid) Duke's rug in its usual location.
13. A relieved Duke instantly (lay, laid) down and closed his eyes.
14. As for Fiffi, she was once again able to (lay, lie) peacefully on the window seat in the sunshine.
15. Mr. McGregor (laid, lay) in his recliner and watched the football game.

Name ______________________

Set the Table, Sit for Tea

> The verb **sit** means to assume a sitting position or to occupy a seat. The principal parts of *sit* are *sit, sat, (have, has, had) sat.* The verb **set** means to put something in position or to make something rigid. The principal parts of *set* are *set, set, (have, has, had) set.*
>
> ***sit:*** *She likes to **sit** in the chair by the window.*
> ***set:*** *She **set** her tea on the ledge by the window.*

Circle the correct verb in each of the following sentences.

1. Claire and I (sat, set) aside some time to spend with Mrs. Fargate, the widow who lives next door.
2. We had (sat, set) out our best clothes for the occasion.
3. When we arrived, Mrs. Fargate asked us to come in and (set, sit) down.
4. Several ceramic pots filled with coral-colored geraniums were (sat, set) on the window ledge to create a happy atmosphere.
5. I (sat, set) in an overstuffed chair with green-and-white-checked cushions and looked around.
6. Clarie chose to (set, sit) upon a fluffy couch.
7. Mrs. Fargate's miniature poodle, Teacup, (sat, set) politely on the rocking chair, showing off the pink ribbon attached to the curly hair on her forehead.
8. We (sat, set) there together talking about trivial things.
9. Mrs. Fargate (sat, set) out the dishes.
10. She served us frosted lemon bars, which she (sat, set) on lovely linen napkins.
11. Our hostess (sat, set) a fine white porcelain teapot, decorated with tiny painted roses, on the coffee table.
12. Then she poured the tea into the delicate little cups that had been (sat, set) out for our visit.
13. Mrs. Fargate moved elegantly, (setting, sitting) her cup gently in the saucer.
14. We had a wonderful time (sitting, setting) in Mrs. Fargate's sunny parlor.

Name ______________________________

Accepting Effective Exceptions

Don't confuse the meaning of these troublesome verbs.

accept: (v) to take what is offered
except: (prep) to leave out; other than

affect: (v) to influence; change
effect: (n) result; consequence

*We will **accept** the invitation.*
*Everyone **except** Joe is going.*

*The weather may **affect** our plans.*
*Hopefully, the **effect** will be good.*

Circle the correct verb to complete each of the following sentences.

On the Beat

1. Police officers (accept, except) the responsibility of enforcing the law of the land.
2. Their commitment to the job can drastically (affect, effect) the community.
3. A policeman is a friend to everyone (accept, except) the lawbreaker.
4. Going to prison is one possible (affect, effect) of committing a crime.

Green Grass of Home

1. Yes, I am willing to (accept, except) payment for a job well done.
2. I always charge at least $10.00 when I mow a lawn, (accept, except) when I mow Mrs. Kennedy's for free.
3. Rain (affects, effects) how quickly the grass grows.
4. The (affect, effect) of lots of rain is a lot of lawn-mowing work for me.

A Good Example

1. I don't mind babysitting my little sister, (accept, except) when I have other plans.
2. Since she doesn't like anyone else to watch her, babysitting my sister has begun to (affect, effect) my social life.
3. My mom always tells me that I have a good (affect, effect) on my little sister.
4. I guess I can (accept, except) that.

Brain Power

1. (Accept, Except) for Saturday and Sunday, I go to school every day.
2. All of this studying is starting to (affect, effect) my brain.
3. It's difficult for me to (accept, except) the fact that I have to study before a test.
4. But when I do, the (affect, effect) is that I usually get a good grade.

Name ______________________

Go Down, Moses

> A **direct object** is a noun, a pronoun, or a group of words acting as a noun that receives the action of the verb. It is easy to find the direct object by asking the question *what* or *whom* after the verb.
>
> *In seventh grade we study* ***heroes****.*
> *Ask: We study* ***whom****?* *Answer:* ***heroes***

Read the sentences about Harriet Tubman and circle the direct objects. Some sentences may have more than one direct object, while other sentences may have none.

1. The courageous Harriet Tubman freed many slaves by way of the underground railroad.
2. Harriet would sing an old spiritual as a signal to the slaves to leave.
3. She was called Moses because many thought she was similar to the biblical figure.
4. The slaves would escape from the plantations in the middle of the night.
5. They desperately wanted freedom.
6. The band of fugitives traveled by foot from their southern states toward Canada.
7. While the runaways walked, Harriet told them vivid stories about freedom to calm their growing fears.
8. Many brave men and women helped to hide the fugitives on their flight to freedom.
9. Fortunately, Harriet Tubman never lost any passengers on her 19 trips on the underground railroad.
10. People issued rewards totaling $40,000 for the capture of Harriet Tubman.
11. As a spy during the Civil War, she freed more than 750 slaves.
12. Harriet Tubman risked her life to lead hundreds of men, women, and children to freedom.

Name ____________________

Happily Ever After

An **indirect object** is a noun or pronoun that names the person *to whom* or *for whom* something is done. To find the indirect object, ask *to whom* or *for whom* after the action verb.

The Prince sang Cinderella an off-key love song.
Question: The Prince sang an off-key love song ***to whom****?*
Answer: Cinderella

In each of the following sentences, underline the indirect object and circle the action verb. Write the title of the fairy tale to which each sentence is referring in the corresponding box below.

1. She was bringing her grandmother a basket of goodies.
2. A man sold the little pig a bundle of sticks for building a house.
3. She left Baby Bear an empty porridge bowl.
4. They worked hard each night to make the shoemaker some leather shoes.
5. The wicked stepmother gave her many chores to do.
6. The pea hidden beneath the pile of mattresses gave her a sore back.
7. He handed his mother the magic beans.
8. The tailors made the emperor royal new garments.
9. She gave the wicked witch a push into the hot oven.
10. The handsome prince gave Sleeping Beauty a kiss to awaken her.
11. The wicked queen, dressed as an old hag, offered the girl a poisonous apple.
12. The tricky trio told the troll a lie.

1.	2.	3.	4.	5.	6.
7.	8.	9.	10.	11.	12.

Name ______________________________

Collection Craze

The noun or pronoun used as the **object of the preposition** follows the preposition or prepositional phrase. A preposition relates the noun or pronoun to another word in the sentence. To find the object of the preposition, ask *whom* or *what* after the preposition.

Lucinda jumped over the gate.

Lucinda jumped over what? ***the gate***

Grandma sent money to us.

Grandma sent money to whom? ***us***

Read the paragraphs below. Place parentheses around the prepositional phrases and underline the objects of the preposition. Find 23 objects of the preposition.

It seems that everyone collects something these days. For some reason, collecting has become one of America's most popular hobbies. Aside from ordinary stamp or coin collecting, individuals of all ages are collecting everything from unique pencil erasers to the ever-popular stuffed animals. Baseball cards have been highly collectible for many years, but today a person can collect any kind of card, including basketball, football, hockey, and even post cards. Books, cars, shoes, teacups, hats—a collector's possibilities are endless.

Many people are willing to spend a great deal of money on their collections. A rare baseball card could cost a collector thousands of dollars. Doll collectors often spend hundreds of dollars for a single, yet desirable, piece for their collection. Without a doubt, these collectors hope that over many years their treasures will increase in value.

In addition to expensive collectibles, there are many that cost the collector nothing except time and effort. Some people keep greeting cards or snippets of wrapping paper received on gifts. Shells, rocks, feathers, leaves, and other items from nature are common collector's items. Matchbooks from restaurants are also freebie collectibles. Collecting one's favorite things is fun, regardless of their true value. So, join the collecting craze. After all, everybody's doing it!

Name ______________________________

Gunky Goop

Compound prepositions are two or more words working together like a one-word preposition.

*The skiers **in front of** the fireplace were drinking hot chocolate.*

Read the advertisement for GUNKY GOOP and underline each compound preposition.

And now, a word from our sponsors . . .

According to cool kids everywhere, *GUNKY GOOP* finishes ahead of all other hair gels. Squeeze a dab of *GUNKY GOOP* out of its funky tube and you'll be blown away by its fun, fresh scent. Create crazy styles in addition to shiny looks when you use *GUNKY GOOP*. Because of its mighty holding power, *GUNKY GOOP* will keep your hair looking fine for hours. Say goodbye to geeky hair styles and bad hair days forever! Instead of using other lame gels, try *GUNKY GOOP*.

GUNKY GOOP . . .
GEL FOR KIDS WHO KNOW COOL.

List the six compound prepositions that you found.

1. ______________________________
2. ______________________________
3. ______________________________
4. ______________________________
5. ______________________________
6. ______________________________

Name ______________________________

The World of Greek Mythology

A **prepositional phrase** is a group of words that shows how two words or ideas are related to each other. It can function as an adjective or an adverb, depending on the word it modifies. Like a one-word adjective, an **adjective prepositional phrase** modifies only a noun or a pronoun.

*One ancient myth **about the rainbow goddess named Iris** captivated my attention.*

In the following sentences, underline the adjective prepositional phrases and draw an arrow to the word being modified. Make sure the prepositional phrase modifies a noun.

1. Ancient Greek stories about gods and goddesses are called myths.
2. Myths from the Greek world were created to explain the mysteries of nature.
3. Poseidon, god of the sea, was also god of earthquakes and horses.
4. The world of mythology is filled with gods, goddesses, and mortals with many marvelous powers.
5. The *Iliad* and the *Odyssey*, by Homer, contain most of the main mythological characters and themes.
6. Eros, from ancient mythology, assisted many in their quest for love.
7. Mount Olympus was the home of the major Greek gods and goddesses.
8. Zeus was a powerful Olympian in the sky and ruled over all the gods.
9. Aphrodite was known as the goddess of love and beauty.
10. Hades' home in the underworld was the land of the dead.
11. Apollo was very strong and was known as the god of music, poetry, and purity.
12. Messages for the gods were delivered by Hermes, who was swift in flight.

Name ______________________________

The White House

Like a one-word adverb, an **adverb prepositional phrase** usually modifies a verb and may tell *where, how,* or *when* an action takes place.

The White House is located ***in Washington, D.C.*** (tells where)
The president resides there ***with his family members****.* (tells how)
He will leave the White House ***at the end of his term****.* (tells when)

In the following sentences, underline the adverb prepositional phrases and circle the words being modified. At the end of each sentence, write whether it tells **where**, **how**, or **when** the action takes place.

1. The West Wing was completed in 1909 and includes the new oval office.
2. Since 1934, the Oval Office has served as the president's formal office.
3. The president and the first lady entertain guests in the East Room.
4. Inside the Green Room, which he used as a dining area, Thomas Jefferson placed a green cloth on the floor.
5. The Green Room became a sitting room when it was decorated with green furnishings.
6. The Blue Room was named by Martin Van Buren, the 8th president.
7. The 19th-century president Rutherford B. Hayes took the oath of office in the Red Room, which is used today as a sitting room.
8. Before state dinners, the president often entertains foreign leaders in the Yellow Oval Room.
9. In 1941, the executive wing replaced a greenhouse complex.
10. In the Lincoln Bedroom, the Emancipation Proclamation was signed by President Lincoln.
11. On the second floor, the Lincoln Sitting Room adjoins the Lincoln Bedroom.
12. A library containing many books is positioned on the ground floor.

Name ____________________

Amazing Advertisements

Adjectives modify (or describe) nouns. They answer the questions *which one, what kind,* or *how many.*

*Mike's dog wears a **black leather** collar around his neck.*

Read the labels from the products below. Underline the adjectives that describe each product.

Energizer
a delicious,
vitamin-filled

CHEWY AND CHOCOLATEY
MONSTER CHUNK
A thick block of
dark chocolate and caramel

Jazzy
Jewel
Amazing Nail
Polish
Glittery royal
colors
to make your
fingernails
sparkle like
beautiful gems!

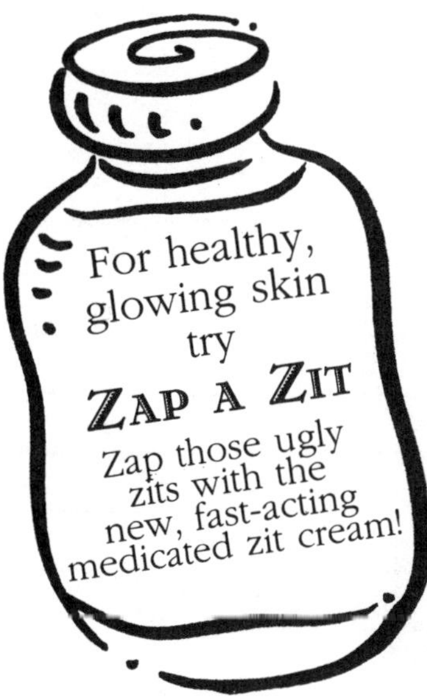

For healthy,
glowing skin
try
ZAP A ZIT
Zap those ugly
zits with the
new, fast-acting
medicated zit cream!

Name ______________________________

Who's Better?

A **comparative adjective** or **adverb** is used to describe a comparison between two things, people, places, or actions. A **superlative adjective** or **adverb** compares three or more things, people, places, or actions.

	positive	***comparative***	***superlative***
adjectives	*happy*	*happier*	*happiest*
	good	*better*	*best*
adverbs	*happily*	*more/less happily*	*most/least happily*
	well	*better*	*best*

Add the comparative and superlative forms of each adjective and adverb to the charts below.

Adjectives

Positive	Comparative	Superlative
new		
durable		
cheap		
big		
comfortable		
beautiful		
creative		

Adverbs

Positive	Comparative	Superlative
proudly		
courageously		
quickly		
easily		
cheerfully		
safely		
slowly		

Name ______________________________

Touring the Zoo

This, **that**, **these**, and **those** are adjectives that modify nouns by telling *which one* or *which ones. This* and *that* are singular. *These* and *those* are plural. *This* and *these* refer to things nearby, and *that* and *those* refer to things farther away.

__This__ zoo we are visiting is the best in the state.
__That__ zoo across town isn't nearly as nice.
__These__ animals we are seeing are cared for very well.
__Those__ animals over there are not cared for very well.

Circle the correct form of each adjective in each of the following sentences.

1. To your immediate right you will see (this, these) beautiful pink flamingos.
2. Just past the trees are (these, those) peacocks displaying their elaborately decorated tail feathers.
3. (That, This) bald eagle nesting in the exhibit next to you has recently hatched an eaglet.
4. Here inside this building we see (these, those) handsome penguins swimming in the frigid water.
5. Over there you will see (these, those) marvelous white polar bears resting on the ice.
6. Right in front of you is (this, these) special sea lion and her cub.
7. Let's head back outside to see (these, those) fantastic big cats.
8. Here we see (this, these) sleeping lions.
9. Further down are (these, those) pacing tigers.
10. And way over there is (this, that) breathtaking snow leopard.
11. At the petting zoo, we will see (these, those) pigs rolling in the mud.
12. (This, That) flock of sheep will feel soft and woolly to the touch.
13. Inside (this, that) next part of the zoo, we see alligators sunning themselves.
14. Before we go, let's stop just ahead and watch (these, those) monkeys clown around.
15. Here we are near our last and largest zoo animal—(this, that) remarkable African elephant.

Name ______________________________

Get Your Popcorn Here!

This, that, these, and *those* are **demonstrative adjectives** that point out a particular person, place, or thing. Use *this* and *these* for things close by and *that* and *those* for things distant in time or space. *This* and *that* are singular while *these* and *those* are plural.

Look at ***that*** *popcorn.* (singular, far)
Look at ***this*** *popcorn.* (singular, near)
Look at ***those*** *candy bars.* (plural, far)
Look at ***these*** *candy bars.* (plural, near)

Underline the demonstrative adjectives and the words they modify. Then, write each treat under the proper category below.

1. I'd like some of this cotton candy, please.
2. I'm not interested in those bags of peanuts.
3. Could you help me carry these cups of soda?
4. This pack of gummy pandas will keep my little brother happy.
5. Please grab that box of chocolates for me.
6. Look at those huge buckets of popcorn!
7. Before we go sit down, I think I'll take that box of spiced candy.
8. I think we should share these candy bars.

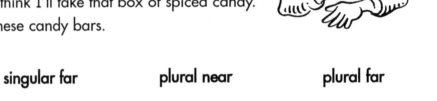

singular near	singular far	plural near	plural far
____________	____________	____________	____________
____________	____________	____________	____________

An **indefinite adjective** is an adjective that gives an approximate number or quantity. It does not tell exactly how many or how much.

When we go to the movies, we buy a ***few*** *snacks to share with each other.*

In the following sentences, underline the indefinite adjectives.

1. When many friends go to the theater with me, we buy more snacks and pass them around.
2. Each person in the group buys something different to pass.
3. Some friends choose candy.
4. Of course, many people prefer to buy salty snacks to eat.
5. Soda pop is usually purchased by several movie goers.
6. After the movie, all snackers feel a little sick to their stomachs.

Name ______________________________

Greenville Is on the Map

A **proper adjective** is an adjective formed from a proper noun. It is always capitalized and may contain more than one word.

***California** girls* ***Memorial Day** parade*

Underline and capitalize all the proper adjectives from this list of locations in the small town of Greenville.

jordan's grove	apple tree	yellow house
stop sign	soccer field	high school
mexican restaurant	pumpkin patch	grocery store
chinese food	bradford's creek	new church
patsy's pond	joe's mail truck	flower shop
flower garden	greenville library	fix-it shop
beauty salon	italian ice shop	dairy farm
siamese cat	vegetable stand	american bank
dr. dan's office	department store	shoe shop

Add at least one proper adjective, formed from a proper noun, for each of the items below.

1. ______________________________ surf shop
2. ______________________________ bowling alley
3. ______________________________ beach
4. ______________________________ station
5. ______________________________ dog

Name ______________________

Spelunking

A **predicate adjective** follows a linking verb and describes the subject.

Lanora's flashlight ***is*** *bright.*

In each of the following sentences, underline the linking verb and circle the predicate adjective(s). Then draw an arrow from the predicate adjective to the subject it modifies.

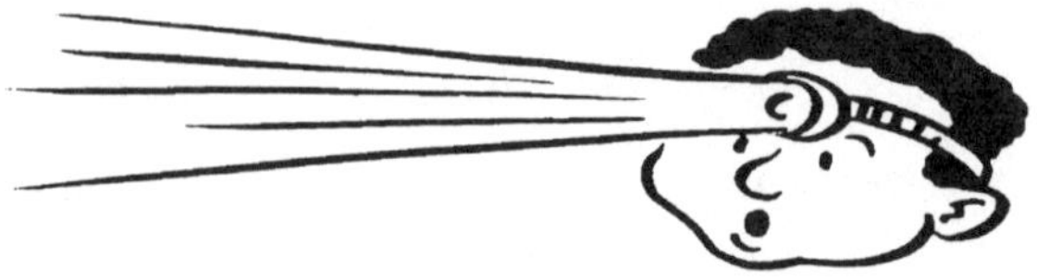

1. The cave was cold and damp.
2. Deep inside the cave it was pitch dark, and we had to use flashlights to see where we were going.
3. Although a litter of bats hanging above us was intimidating, none came near us.
4. The stalactites overhead were wet.
5. They were shiny and beautiful, like icicles.
6. The stalagmites growing out of the cave floor were equally amazing.
7. Droplets of water falling into the nearby pools were surprisingly noisy in the quiet cave.
8. Several areas of the cave were still unexplored.
9. Our tour was very informative.
10. Underground caves are thrilling!

For each illustration below, write a sentence containing a subject, a linking verb, and a predicate adjective.

1. ______________________

2. ______________________

3. ______________________

4. ______________________

5. ______________________

Name ______________________________

Proverbs to Ponder

The three **articles** are *a, an,* and *the*. Articles are adjectives and always come before a noun. *A* and *an* are indefinite, singular articles, referring to any one of a class of nouns. The article *an* always comes before a word that begins with a vowel or a vowel sound. *A* comes before a word that begins with a consonant. *The* is definite and refers to a specific noun. It can be singular or plural.

an *ideal place* ***a*** *simple little story* ***the*** *most amazing person*

In each of the proverbs below, fill in the blank with the correct article.

1. Birds of _______ feather flock together.
2. Too many cooks spoil _______ broth.
3. You can't teach _______ old dog new tricks.
4. _______ early bird catches _______ worm.
5. One tree doesn't make _______ forest.
6. Every cloud has _______ silver lining.
7. _______ apple _______ day keeps _______ doctor away.
8. If _______ shoe fits, wear it.
9. _______ picture is worth _______ thousand words.
10. Strike while _______ iron is hot.

Write the correct article, *a* or *an,* in front of the nouns.

_____ actor	_____ wreath	_____ evening	_____ tragedy
_____ beauty	_____ hospital	_____ orchestra	_____ honor
_____ answer	_____ camera	_____ hammer	_____ ink pen
_____ outrage	_____ omen	_____ pleasure	_____ ego

Name ____________________

A Really Bad Beginning

Good and **bad** are adjectives that modify nouns. **Well** and **badly** are adverbs that modify verbs.

That was a ***good*** *shot.* (adjective) *He shot at that* ***well****.* (adverb)
That was a ***bad*** *shot.* (adjective) *He shot at that* ***badly****.* (adverb)

Select the correct modifier in each of the following sentences.

When I woke up this morning I was feeling quite (good, well). I went to the sink to give myself a (good, well) teeth-brushing, but when I glanced into the mirror I saw it. There, on my forehead, was a huge red pimple, and it looked really (bad, badly). I immediately dropped my toothbrush and reached for a comb. I tried combing my bangs straight down over the ugly thing, but that didn't work too (good, well). Then I tried sticking a round band-aid over it, but that didn't look very (good, well) either. A sick sensation came over me; I felt (bad, badly).

Maybe I could pop it, I thought, but decided that I might hurt myself too (bad, badly). A (good, well) cover-up might work. So, next I tried my mom's make-up stick, which worked pretty (good, well), if you consider a big brown bump in the middle of your forehead a (good, well) thing. As a last resort, I threw on my favorite hat, which hid the nasty zit fairly (good, well). The (bad, badly) thing is that hats aren't allowed in any of my classes. I wished so (bad, badly) that I could just stay home. I had a feeling it wasn't going to be a very (good, well) day at all.

Name ____________________

The Prince Frog

An **adverb** is a word that modifies a verb, an adjective, or another adverb. Adverbs indicate **time**, **place**, or **manner**. **Adverbs of time** answer the questions *when* or *how often*. **Adverbs of place** answer the question *where*. **Adverbs of manner** answer the questions *how* or *in what manner*.

time: *Camilla slept* ***late****.*
place: *Camilla slept* ***here****.*
manner: *Camilla slept* ***soundly****.*

For every circled verb in the story, underline the corresponding adverb. Write the adverbs in the appropriate columns below.

Once upon a time, Camilla the frog (lived) alone in the swamp near King Ronald's castle. From her lily pad she could plainly (see) the bridge that crossed the moat surrounding the castle. Day after day, while skillfully (catching) her afternoon meal of flies, Camilla always (daydreamed) about life in a royal's world. She often (dreamt) of princesses in beautiful gowns gaily (strolling) through elegant flower gardens while young princes lazily (rested) on plush cushions by inviting little ponds. On this particular morning, Camilla decided (to venture) slowly over and finally (get) a glimpse of royal life.

Hopping across was long and difficult under the heat of the rising sun. But when she (arrived) there, Camilla instantly (saw) an unexpected and amazing sight. Under a pear-filled tree, a charming prince (lay) asleep. He was tall, dark, and handsomely (dressed) in green from head to toe. Immediately Camilla (swooned) and (drooled) as she watched the perfect creature (sleeping) nearby. Next, Camilla (leapt) to within inches of his princely face when suddenly he (stirred). She quickly (grabbed) her chance. In one move, she (jumped) up and kissed him on the lips. The dashing prince instantly (transformed) into a bumpy green frog. An elated Camilla gasped, "Here you are, my wonderful prince frog!"

Manner		Time		Place
________	________	________	________	________
________	________	________	________	________
________	________	________		________
________	________	________		________
________				

Name ______________________

A Close Call

Adverbs have three degrees of comparison. They are positive, comparative, and superlative. Some adverbs form the comparative degree by adding ***er*** and the superlative degree by adding ***est***. Most adverbs that end in *ly* form their comparative degrees by adding the words ***more*** or ***less*** in front of the positive degree. The superlative degree is formed by adding the words ***most*** or ***least*** in front of the positive degree.

Raquel danced less gracefully then her sisters.
I hope they will come sooner rather than later.

Write the missing adverbs in the chart.

Positive	Comparative	Superlative
fast	faster	fastest
carefully	more/less carefully	most/least carefully
soon		
hard		
noisily		
late		
easily		
efficiently		
loudly		
softly		
harshly		
neatly		
cheerfully		
courageously		
correctly		

In the following sentences, circle the adverbs and indicate the degree of comparison: **P** (positive), **C** (comparative), or **S** (superlative).

____ 1. The principal walks quickly through the halls.
____ 2. David plans more intelligently than the other boys.
____ 3. He dives the most gracefully behind the bleachers.
____ 4. One boy leaps the least deftly and falls on his behind.
____ 5. The third boy, diving more quickly than the second, makes it with only one leg hanging out.
____ 6. Walking slowly across the gym floor, the principal notices the stray leg.
____ 7. Hopping faster than a cricket, she pounces on the leg, pulling the boy from his spot.
____ 8. David, creeping most carefully behind the bleachers, escapes to skip school another day.

double negatives

Name ______________________

Negative Norman

A **double negative** incorrectly uses two negative words when one is sufficient. Use only one negative when you mean to say "no."

Noelle didn't want no macaroni. (incorrect)
Noelle didn't want any macaroni. (correct)

Cross out the double negatives in the following sentences. Then, rewrite each sentence so that it does not contain a double negative.

1. Negative Norman never seems to like nothing.
____
2. On Saturday mornings when his mom makes him pancakes, he says, "I don't want none!"
____
____
3. When his buddies from school call, he will not talk to no one.
____
____
4. Norman is so nasty he won't even feed his dog no food.
____
5. All day he just sits in his bean bag chair and won't never go nowhere.
____
____
6. Norman doesn't seem to have no smile at all.
____
7. He obviously hasn't learned nothing about enjoying life.
____
8. No one can never make no comments about his negativity neither.
____
____
9. Norman isn't interested in no know-it-all's opinions about his attitude.
____
____
10. Negative Norman doesn't want no friends, no fun, nor no advice from nobody.
____
____

Name ______________________________

Ancient Pyramids

The complete subject or complete predicate of a sentence usually contains other words or phrases, called **modifiers**, that add to the meaning of the sentence.

*The ancient tombs, **which stand powerfully on the hot sands of Egypt**, are an amazing and wonderful sight.*

In the following sentences, underline the subject modifiers once and the predicate modifiers twice.

1. Ancient pyramids stand majestically in the golden desert sands of Egypt.
2. The Egyptian pyramids were erected nearly five thousand years ago.
3. Skilled craftsmen and unskilled laborers worked together to build the pyramids.
4. Brilliant architects carefully calculated and thoughtfully designed the pyramids.
5. The dangerous, difficult work of building pyramids was done slowly and carefully.
6. These incredibly large structures were built especially for the pharaohs.
7. Ancient Egyptians believed wholeheartedly in life after death.
8. The bodies of dead kings were effectively preserved and buried in the tombs.
9. Food, clothing, furniture, and jewelry that the deceased Pharaoh would need in the afterlife were buried with him.
10. Each pyramid would protect the body.
11. The embalmed body of King Khufu was once enshrined in the Great Pyramid of Giza.
12. Young King Tutankhamen was buried in royal fashion within a tomb in the Valley of the Kings.

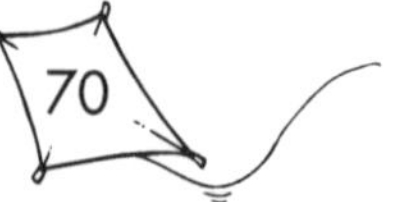

Name ______________________________

Locked Out

Modifiers that are not placed near the words or phrases that they modify are called **misplaced modifiers**.

> ***Scared to death***, *the black night enveloped the lost student. (misplaced modifier)*
>
> ***Scared to death***, *the lost student wandered the neighborhood in abandon. (correct)*

Underline the misplaced modifiers in the following sentences. Then, rewrite each sentence correctly.

1. After school, I have a key for getting into our locked house.

   ____

   ____

2. Under the flower pot I always know I can find an extra key.

   ____

   ____

3. The flower pot is missing unfortunately.

   ____

   ____

4. In the basement, I consider breaking a window.

   ____

   ____

5. On the roof, I think about going down the chimney.

   ____

   ____

6. Instead, I sit on the porch and wait for my mom to get home for an hour.

   ____

   ____

7. We discover that the door had not even been locked when she arrives.

   ____

   ____

8. The dog barks at us as we go in through the window.

   ____

   ____

Name ______________________________

Sand and Surf

> If a modifying word, phrase, or clause does not modify a particular word, then it is called a **dangling modifier**. Every modifier must have a word that it clearly modifies.
>
> *Warmed by the sun, it felt good to be at the beach.*
> *(dangling modifier—"warmed by the sun" does not modify **it**)*
>
> *Warmed by the sun, we thought a day at the beach felt good.*
> *(correct—"warmed by the sun" does modify **we**)*

In the following sentences, underline the dangling modifier and draw an arrow to the word it is incorrectly modifying. If the modifier is used correctly, write **OK** in the blank.

_____ 1. While running down to the water, the sand was too hot.

_____ 2. Surrounded by a moat, I created a masterpiece.

_____ 3. Under the umbrella, the picnic basket filled with snack foods sat.

_____ 4. Reclining on the beach, sunscreen is extremely important.

_____ 5. With too much sun, many sunbathers will burn.

Rewrite these sentences, correcting the dangling modifiers.

1. Riding the big waves, excited shouts emerge from the water.

____

____

2. Lying in the sun, my suntan lotion didn't work.

____

____

3. Playing barefoot, the volleyball game took place on the hot sand.

____

____

4. Tired and sandy, our beach day ended.

____

____

5. Hanging out at the beach, the time was a lot of fun.

____

____

Name ______________________

Star-Crossed Lovers

A **participle** is a verb form that can function as an adjective. The **present participle** is usually formed by adding ***ing*** to a present tense verb. The **past participle** is usually formed by adding ***ed*** to the present tense. A **participial phrase** is a group of words that includes the participle and its objects, complements, or modifiers.

present participle: *Rex barks at the* ***passing*** *cars.*
past participle: *A* ***determined*** *Rex tried to chase the car.*

In each of the following sentences, identify if the participle used is a present (**P**) or a past (**PA**) participle.

_____ 1. Romeo's parents enquire about their moping son.

_____ 2. Discovering Rosaline's name on the guest list, Benvolio encourages Romeo to "crash" the Capulet party.

_____ 3. Wearing a mask, Romeo arrives at the party.

_____ 4. There he sees the smiling Juliet and longs to meet her.

_____ 5. The dancing couple fall hopelessly in love.

_____ 6. Struck by love, Juliet is distressed to learn that Romeo belongs to the house of Montague.

_____ 7. The feuding Montagues and Capulets hate each other.

_____ 8. Appearing on the balcony, Juliet declares her passion for Romeo.

_____ 9. Overheard by Romeo, her words of love inspire him.

_____ 10. Soon, a determined Romeo appeals to the friar to marry the couple immediately.

_____ 11. Standing before the friar, the young lovers are married in secret.

_____ 12. Later, Romeo finds the quarreling Benvolio and Mercutio in the public square and ultimately kills Tybalt.

_____ 13. Romeo is banished to Mantua while a mourning Juliet seeks help from the friar.

_____ 14. Committed to being reunited with her husband, Juliet carries out a dangerous plan.

_____ 15. Deceived by his sleeping lover, Romeo drinks the poison.

_____ 16. An awakening Juliet discovers her dying Romeo and tragically stabs herself to join him in death.

Name ______________________________

Chores

A **gerund** is a verb form ending in *ing* that functions as a noun. Gerunds are formed by adding *ing* to the present tense verb form. A **gerund phrase** is a group of words that includes a gerund and its related words.

gerund: ***Dancing*** *is my favorite form of exercise.*
gerund phrase: ***Dancing the polka*** *is a good workout.*

In each of the following sentences, underline the gerund or gerund phrase and indicate how it is being used in the sentence: **S** (subject), **DO** (direct object), **OP** (object of a preposition), or **PN** (predicate noun).

_____ 1. Cleaning is the worst job.

_____ 2. I prefer cooking.

_____ 3. Sometimes I avoid my chores by complaining.

_____ 4. Another strategy is procrastinating.

_____ 5. Vacuuming isn't so bad.

_____ 6. I hate dusting.

_____ 7. Occasionally, the windows need washing.

_____ 8. Mopping makes the floors shine.

_____ 9. My room appears messy when the bed needs making.

_____ 10. Mowing the lawn can be relaxing work.

_____ 11. I'm not fond of pulling weeds when it is scorching hot outside.

_____ 12. Washing dishes is a job my sister and I share.

_____ 13. A disgusting chore is scrubbing the toilet.

_____ 14. We never worry about polishing the silver.

_____ 15. Feeding the cat has been my little brother's only chore.

_____ 16. Everyone in our house is responsible for folding laundry.

_____ 17. Dad mainly likes fixing things.

_____ 18. The best part of a chore is finishing the job.

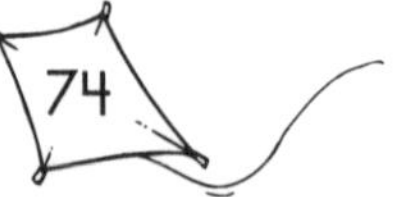

Name ______________________________

Medieval Times

Use a comma to separate an **introductory phrase** or **clause** from the rest of the sentence. Oftentimes these phrases will contain a preposition.

Because I am sick, I will not be able to attend the medieval festival at the park.

Underline the introductory phrase or clause in each of the following sentences. Then, add the proper punctuation to each one.

1. During the Middle Ages the European form of government was feudalism.
2. At that time in European history there were many fiefs, estates of feudal lords.
3. In return for his loyalty a nobleman was provided with land by the king.
4. Under the feudal system the owner of a fief was often a lord whose land was inhabited by people who promised to serve him.
5. When a person controlled land he also had political, economic, judicial, and military power.
6. At the age of about seven many young boys left home to train for knighthood.
7. As soon as a squire had mastered the necessary skills he became a knight.
8. As a knight a nobleman was a soldier for the king when necessary.
9. Because they had few rights peasants were at the mercy of their lords.
10. In return for clerical services many lords gave fiefs to the church.

Write an introductory phrase or clause for each of the following sentence endings. Add the proper punctuation.

1. ______________________________ preparations for the feast began.
2. ______________________________ the manor had to be cleaned.
3. ______________________________ large amounts of elaborate foods were prepared.
4. ______________________________ trumpets announced the arrival of the king.
5. ______________________________ all the guests enjoyed a feast fit for a king.

Name ____________________

At the Carnival

An **independent clause** is a group of words with a subject and a predicate that expresses a complete thought and can stand by itself as a sentence. A **dependent clause** cannot stand alone. It depends upon the independent clause of the sentence to complete its meaning. Dependent clauses start with words like *who, which, that, because, when, if, until, before,* and *after.*

dependent clause — independent clause

When we went to the school carnival, we witnessed many pranks.

Draw a line from each independent clause to a dependent clause to form a new sentence.

The teacher fell into the dunk tank	because she had a "kick-me" sign stuck to her back.
Her face turned bright red	after their canoe was tipped over.
The pie hit her in the face	when the baseball hit the target.
After he fell asleep,	they sprayed shaving cream all over his head.
All the girls screamed	while he was not looking.
He was so embarrassed	when she saw her undies being strung up the flagpole.
They put a worm on his plate	that he couldn't speak.
Everyone laughed	when he threw it.

The sentences below each have a dependent and an independent clause. Underline the dependent clause once and the independent twice.

1. Janie was sad because she didn't have enough money to go on the Ferris wheel.
2. After Jack ate two bags of cotton candy, he felt sick.
3. While Mrs. Brown wasn't looking, two kids snuck into the Tunnel O' Love.
4. The girls all cheered when the carnival strongman lifted two grown men over his head.

Name ______________________________

Claws

An **adjective clause** is a dependent clause that functions as an adjective. It can modify any noun or pronoun in a sentence. Adjective clauses tell *which one, what kind,* or *how many.*

*Some of the animals **that live in the wild** have claws.*

In each of the following sentences, underline each adjective clause and circle the word it modifies.

1. Feline claws, which are used to catch prey, are retractable.
2. An owl's claws, which are called talons, are dangerous weapons.
3. Rather than claws, orangutans possess fingers that have fingerprints much like a human's.
4. A polar bear uses his front paws and short, sharp claws for holding on to prey that is slippery.
5. There are five fingers on a panda's hand and five toes on each foot, which all have long, sharp claws.
6. Playful lion cubs, who must learn to hunt, use their claws to snag anything that moves.
7. The hoof of a giraffe, which has no claws, makes a print larger than a dinner plate.
8. The fishing bat, which hunts fish swimming near the water's surface, swoops down and uses its long claws to grab the fish.
9. With her back legs, the female turtle digs a hole that she will use to protect her eggs.
10. A parrot has two toes that point forward and two toes that point backward.
11. Wolf babies are born underground in dens that are often dug by the wolves' parents.
12. Claws that are found on the feet of birds, reptiles, and mammals are often sharp, hooked structures.
13. A dog's toenails, which grow long, need to be cut regularly.
14. All claws, nails, talons, horns, and hoofs are made of the same material, which is hardened cells of the epidermis, the outer layer of skin.

Name ______________________________

Santa Claus

An **adverb clause** is a dependent clause that functions as an adverb. It can modify a verb, an adjective, or another adverb. Adverb clauses tell *how, where, when,* or *why* an action happened.

It seems nearly everyone believes in Santa ***when they are very young****.*

In each of the following sentences, underline the adverb clause, circle the word or phrase it modifies, and write the question it answers: *how, when, where,* or *why.*

_____ 1. Santa arrives on Christmas Eve.

_____ 2. Santa flies with the speed of light.

_____ 3. Santa enters the room by coming down the chimney with a bound.

_____ 4. On his back, he carries a bag full of toys.

_____ 5. Up on the rooftop, the reindeer wait.

_____ 6. Santa sits by the fireplace and reads a note the children left.

_____ 7. Before getting to work, he enjoys the cookies and milk.

_____ 8. Santa didn't eat dinner because he knew there would be a lot of cookies tonight.

_____ 9. After he eats the cookies, he will give the carrots to his reindeer.

_____ 10. The children are fast asleep in their beds.

_____ 11. Because the children have been good all year, Santa will leave their favorite toys.

_____ 12. Santa opens his pack by untying it.

_____ 13. Since some of the children have been naughty, Santa must check his list.

_____ 14. Because they have been bad, Santa fills some children's stockings with coal.

_____ 15. Then, with a twinkle in his eye, he fills the others' stockings with candy and toys.

_____ 16. When he is finished, he lays his finger aside his nose, gives a nod, and goes.

Name ___________________________

Window-Washing Entrepreneurs

A **noun clause** is a dependent clause that functions as a noun. It may be used as a subject, a direct object, an indirect object, an object of a preposition, or a predicate noun.

> ***subject***: ***What occurred*** *was not planned at all.*
> ***direct object***: *They wondered* ***what they should do*** *now.*
> ***indirect object***: *Should they make* ***whoever broke the window*** *pay the bill?*
> ***object of the preposition***: *They were grateful to* ***whoever would clean up the mess.***
> ***predicate noun***: *The good thing was* ***that no one was hurt.***

In each of the following sentences, underline the noun clause and indicate how the clause is used in the sentence: **S** (subject), **DO** (direct object), **IO** (indirect object), **OP** (object of a preposition), or **PN** (predicate noun).

_____ 1. Felix and Frank considered what they could do to earn money.

_____ 2. Felix thought that his idea might work.

_____ 3. What Felix proposed was to start their own window-washing business.

_____ 4. That people would want their windows cleaned seemed obvious to Frank.

_____ 5. How to get the proper equipment was what they had to figure out first.

_____ 6. Then, whatever they could promise to persuade their customers they printed in their advertisement fliers.

_____ 7. They would give whoever called in the first week a discount price.

_____ 8. Felix and Frank agreed that the fliers should be hand-delivered.

_____ 9. Their initial week of washing windows was pretty much what they expected.

_____ 10. Whoever had the dirtiest windows seemed to call for service.

_____ 11. That you should keep your word was their business motto.

_____ 12. So, Felix and Frank gave whoever called a 50 percent discount that first week.

_____ 13. Throughout the summer, they continued to work hard for whomever they could.

_____ 14. That they made some money is certainly true.

_____ 15. They finished the summer feeling proud of that which they had accomplished.

Name ______________________________

Masterpiece in the Snow

An **adjective clause** is a dependent clause that functions as an adjective by telling *what kind* or *which one*. An **adverb clause** is a dependent clause that functions as an adverb. It can modify verbs, adjectives, or other adverbs, and tells *where, when, in what manner, to what extent, under what condition*, or *why*. A **noun clause** is a dependent clause that functions as a noun.

adjective clause**: Building a snowman is one pastime* ***that we enjoy each winter.
adverb clause**: We dress warmly* ***when we play in the snow*.*
noun clause**:* ***What we create out of the snow *is always a labor of love.*

In each of the following sentences, underline the dependent clause and indicate if it is an adjective (**ADJ**), an adverb (**ADV**), or a noun (**N**) clause.

_____ 1. We didn't want to build a snowman that was like all the others.

_____ 2. Every winter we do that.

_____ 3. Today we would create a snowman that no one would forget.

_____ 4. What Craig thought of was perfect!

_____ 5. Build a giant snow monster is what we would do.

_____ 6. The monster grew quickly because the snow packed so well.

_____ 7. The neighbor who lives next door brought a six-foot ladder.

_____ 8. What became the monster's body were packed, giant snowballs.

_____ 9. He grew taller after we hoisted the second ball on top of the first.

_____ 10. To build his height, we added buckets of snow.

_____ 11. Since we were building a giant snow monster, we wanted him to be at least eight feet tall.

_____ 12. When the mound of snow was big enough, we carved out his face and his limbs.

_____ 13. When we stood back and looked, everyone agreed that he wasn't finished.

_____ 14. What he needed was sharp teeth and beady eyes.

_____ 15. Finally, we turned our snowy monster green by spraying him with colored water.

_____ 16. The snow monster that we put so much hard work into is a masterpiece.

Name ______________________________

So Many Sweets

Noun Clauses

In each of the following sentences, underline the noun clause and indicate how the clause is being used in the sentence: **S** (subject), **DO** (direct object), **IO** (indirect object), **OP** (object of the preposition), or **PN** (predicate noun).

_____ 1. Frosted cookies are what make Christmas delicious.

_____ 2. Whoever made this chocolate pie should be kissed.

_____ 3. I hope that this caramel corn isn't stale.

_____ 4. Meg will give whoever says please a giant candy bar.

_____ 5. The cotton candy stuck to all of her fingers.

Adjective Clauses

In each of the following sentences, underline the adjective clause and circle the word it modifies.

1. We buy ice cream from the man who drives the ice-cream truck.
2. The honey that the bees make tastes great on toast.
3. His jawbreaker, which was the size of a golf ball, lasted a long time.
4. Dad and I get doughnuts at the bakery where my cousin works.
5. The fudge maker who worked in town was known for his delicious candy.

Adverb Clauses

In each of the following sentences, underline the adverb clause and write the question it answers: *how, when, where,* or *why.*

_____ 1. You should brush your teeth whenever you've eaten sweets.

_____ 2. My brother is hyperactive because he ate too much Halloween candy.

_____ 3. At Christmastime, we dip candy canes in melted chocolate.

_____ 4. We fondue by dipping strawberries in melted chocolate too.

_____ 5. Lisa and Mike shared a malted milkshake at the ice-cream parlor.

appositives

Name ______________________________

A Bag of Bones

An **appositive** is a noun or noun phrase placed next to or very near another noun or noun phrase to identify, explain, or supplement its meaning, or to rename the initial noun or pronoun.

*Bones, **the scaffolding of the body**, are tied together with ligaments.*

Underline the appositives in each sentence. There may be more than one appositive in each.

1. The cranium, or brain case, is made up of five bones.
2. The clavicle, or collarbone, is a slender, rodlike bone that acts like a brace for the shoulder blade.
3. The shoulder blades, or scapulae, are broad, triangle-shaped bones located on either side of the upper back.
4. A person's breastbone, the sternum, is a flat, elongated bone.
5. Each upper limb of a person's body consists of an upper arm bone, the humerus, and two lower arm bones, the radius and the ulna.
6. Your wrist, or carpus, is composed of eight small carpal bones that are firmly connected in two rows of four bones each.
7. Phlanges, finger and toe bones, play an important role in the body.
8. While in-line skating, John hurt his patella, his knee cap, when he collided with a parked car.
9. The lower leg is formed by two bones, the large tibia and the slender fibula, which extend from the knee to the ankle.
10. The longest bone in the body, the femur, extends from the hip to the knee.
11. Did you know that the seven tarsals that form the heel and the back part of the instep create the tarsus, or the ankle?
12. The smallest bones in the entire body, the malleus, incus, and stapes, connect the eardrum to the inner ear and transmit vibrations from the outer ear to the inner ear.

Name ____________________

That's Amoré!

A **sentence** expresses a complete thought. A sentence must contain a subject and a predicate. Every sentence begins with a capital letter and ends with a period, a question mark, or an exclamation mark.

complete sentence*: My sister eats pizza in bed.*
incomplete sentence*: Pizza in bed.*

Read each sentence below. Before each, write **C** if it is a complete sentence or write **NC** if it is not a complete sentence. If you wrote NC, rewrite the incomplete sentences to create complete ones.

____ 1. It is my turn to make dinner for my family.

____

____ 2. Pizza is it! ____________________

____ 3. First, the dough for the crust. ____________________

____ 4. We like it thick. ____________________

____ 5. I spread the dough evenly into the deep-dish pan.

____

____ 6. Add Grandma's homemade sauce. ____________________

____ 7. It is delicious. ____________________

____ 8. One cup ham, one cup green pepper, and two cups pineapple.

____

____

____ 9. Don't forget the mozzarella. ____________________

____ 10. Lots of cheese on top.

____

____ 11. Bake it. ____________________

____ 12. After thrity mintues at 375°, it is perfect.

____

____ 13. Now we'll eat and enjoy. ____________________

____ 14. Cold pop a must too.

____

____ 15. If there are any leftovers, we will have the rest for breakfast—cold!

____

Name ______________________________

A Sour Experience

The **simple subject** names the person or the object the sentence is about, not including modifying words such as articles (a, an, the) or adjectives. The **simple predicate** tells what the subject is or what the subject does. It is a verb or a verb phrase minus any modifying words.

(simple subject) (simple predicate)

A happy kid munched on sour apples.

(simple subject) (simple predicate)

Mrs. Haggly is taking the apple trees away.

Read the story. Underline the simple subject and circle the simple predicate in each sentence.

The apple trees along Mrs. Haggly's driveway tempted us. From our own yard, we could smell the tartness in the crisp autumn air. Shiny green apples decorated the gnarled old trees. We strained our necks to see them better. Just the thought of biting into one of those apples made our mouths water uncontrollably.

Mrs. Haggly was our only problem. Everyone knew that she was dangerous. She had long wavy white hair and a crooked face. She bent over, using a cane for balance. Many people thought she might even be a witch.

One morning, we decided to make a run for the apples. Boy was that exciting! My brother ran first. I followed. Before we knew it, we had a handful of perfect, little, green apples. Back over the fence we went, quicker than ever! Exhausted and sweating beads of fear, we ate the green apples under the shade of our own tree. They were perfectly sour and delicious!

However, we paid the price for our adventure. Ohhh, did we ache! Our stomachs grew big like watermelons. We were sick all day. This story has a moral. Little green apples are sometimes wicked. Old ladies with canes are usually not.

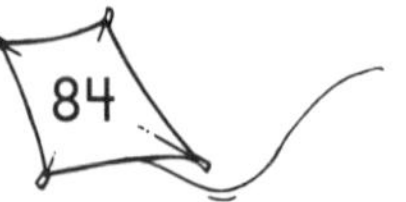

Name ____________________________

Ode to Chocolate

The **complete subject** of a sentence tells what or who the sentence is about and may be one word or many words. The **complete predicate** tells what the subject is or does and may be one word or many words. Both the complete subject and predicate contain articles and modifying words or phrases.

(complete subject) ↘ ↙ (complete predicate)

A cold glass of milk *tastes great after a chocolate-chip cookie.*

In each sentence below, underline the complete subject and circle the complete predicate.

Life would be meaningless without chocolate things.

Chocolate bonbons and clusters would lose all value.

Birthday cakes might as well grow stale without chocolate coverings.

Chocolate cheesecake would lose its character.

Peanut-butter cups would be peanut-butter blobs without their chocolate shells.

Chocolate-free desserts would make no sense at all.

Scoops of ice cream would be desperately lonely.

Chocolate-chip cookies would fall out of style.

Doughnuts for dunking seem ho-hum when the baker forgets the chocolate sprinkles.

Chocolate bunnies would become extinct.

Hot chocolate without the chocolate is just plain stupid, don't you think?

I would have to say,

Chocolate things give life meaning . . . more or less.

Name ______________________________

Autumn and Apples

A **compound subject** is made of two or more subjects that have the same verb and are joined by a conjunction such as *and* or *or*. A **compound predicate** is two or more predicates that have the same subject and are joined by a conjunction.

(compound subject) ↘ ↙(compound predicate)

*My sister **and** I love to make **and** eat caramel apples.*

Underline the compound portion in each of the following sentences. Write **CS** in the blank if it is a compound subject; write **CP** if it is a compound predicate.

____ 1. In the fall, my sister and I always make caramel apples.

____ 2. First, we pick the apples and wash them well.

____ 3. Then, Tami and I melt the caramel squares in the double boiler.

____ 4. If we do not stir the caramels well enough, the mixture will be too chunky and will not work.

____ 5. While we work, Kenneth, our younger brother, eats an apple or sneaks some caramels.

____ 6. Finally, Tami starts dipping and turning the first apple in the hot caramel.

____ 7. Mom and Dad like chopped nuts on their apples.

____ 8. I roll a few apples in the nuts and leave some plain.

____ 9. After dinner, our family will devour and enjoy them for dessert.

____ 10. We love to make caramel apples but hate to clean up the sticky mess and put away all the dishes.

In the following sentences, turn the subject into a compound subject and write the new sentence on the line. You may have to change the verb as well.

1. September is a good time to pick apples.

____

____

2. Deer like to eat apples.

____

____

In the following sentences, turn the predicate into a compound predicate and write the new sentence on the line.

1. Grandma makes apple muffins.

____

____

2. Rotten apples give me a stomachache.

____

____

Name ______________________________

Homework

There are 4 kinds of sentences: **declarative**, **interrogative**, **imperative**, and **exclamatory**.

- **Declarative** sentences make a statement and end with a period.
- **Interrogative** sentences ask a question and end with a question mark.
- **Imperative** sentences command or make a request and end with a period or an exclamation point. ("You" is often the implied subject of the command or request.)
- **Exclamatory** sentences make either a statement or a command with strong feeling and end with an exclamation point.

declarative: *Marcie helps Anne finish her math assignment.*
interrogative: *Does Mike know how to divide decimals?*
imperative: *Please ask him yourself.*
exclamatory: *I need an answer right now!*

Label the following sentences: **D** (declarative), **IN** (interrogative), **IM** (imperative), or **E** (exclamatory). Add the correct punctuation to the end of each sentence.

_____ 1. My teachers always give me too much homework

_____ 2. Don't they know I already have enough to do

_____ 3. Mow the lawn

_____ 4. That's what my dad always says

_____ 5. Did you take out the trash

_____ 6. My mom always wants me to empty the trash cans and take them out to the curb

_____ 7. Sometimes I even have to help my brother with his paper route

_____ 8. Just imagine how tired I get

_____ 9. Can't a guy get a break

_____ 10. Mrs. Barts wants me to do a report about Egyptian mummies, and Mr. Lee suggests I study for the algebra test

_____ 11. What do I know about mummies anyway

_____ 12. Give me a hand with this algebra

_____ 13. I just remembered that I have to rake my grandma's leaves tonight

_____ 14. I've got too much homework

_____ 15. The basketball game is on

Name ______________________________

Shaq

> **Declarative** sentences can be changed to form **interrogative** sentences.
>
> *The basketball is a dull shade of orange.*
> *What color is the basketball?*

Shaquille O'Neal is the slam-dunking star center for the Orlando Magic. Shaq's full name is Shaquille Rashaun O'Neal. His name means "little warrior." Shaquille was born on March 6, 1972. When he was growing up, his parents taught him to value a strong work ethic, wisdom, and responsibility. Shaq's father introduced him to the game of basketball to reinforce these values. Many years later, Shaq went to Louisiana State University to study and to play basketball. He was 17 years old when he began playing college basketball. At that time, he was seven feet one inch (2.2 m) tall and he weighed 290 (132 kg) pounds. Just three years later, Shaq turned pro. The Orlando Magic won the chance to draft him. He began playing in the NBA in 1992.

Change each declarative sentence into an interrogative one.

1. ______________________________
2. ______________________________
3. ______________________________
4. ______________________________
5. ______________________________
6. ______________________________
7. ______________________________
8. ______________________________
9. ______________________________
10. ______________________________
11. ______________________________
12. ______________________________

Name ____________________

Sumo

A **simple sentence** contains one independent clause. (An independent clause contains a subject and a predicate and can stand alone.) A **compound sentence** contains two independent clauses that are closely related. A comma and conjunction or a semicolon usually connects the two clauses.

Maxwell is a sumo wrestler. (simple sentence)
Maxwell trains very hard, but he has never won a competition. (compound sentence)

Put an **S** on the line in front of each simple sentence and a **C** on the line in front of each compound sentence.

_____ 1. Sumo is the national sport of Japan.

_____ 2. There are six major sumo tournaments held each year in Japan, and they attract the attention of the entire nation.

_____ 3. In Japan, a tournament is called a *basho.*

_____ 4. A sumo ring measures 12 feet (3.66m) in diameter and is made of sand and clay.

_____ 5. The goal in sumo wrestling is to either throw your opponent to the ground or to force him out of the ring.

_____ 6. Sumo has no weight classes for competition, and many wrestlers weigh more than 350 pounds (159kg).

_____ 7. The wrestler's big stomach provides him a low center of gravity, and it helps him withstand a charge by his opponent.

_____ 8. Every sumo competition begins with a religious-type ceremony.

_____ 9. Before each match, the competitors clap their hands to awaken the gods, they throw salt into the ring to purify the ground, and they stamp their feet to crush evil.

_____ 10. When the referee gives the signal, the wrestlers take their positions.

_____ 11. They crouch down and place both hands in front of them with their knuckles on the ground.

_____ 12. The highest rank in sumo wrestling is *yokozuna,* which means "grand champion."

Name ______________________________

Butterflies

A **complex sentence** contains an independent clause and one or more dependent clauses. An **independent clause** contains a subject and a predicate and can stand alone. A **dependent clause** has a subject and a predicate, but it cannot stand by itself and still make sense. A dependent clause often begins with a relative pronoun such as *who, which, that, whose,* or *whom.*

> ***independent clause**: The butterfly flitted from flower to flower.*
> ***dependent clause**: whose wings were brightly colored*
> ***complex sentence**: The butterfly, whose wings were brightly colored, flitted from flower to flower.*

Underline the dependent clauses in the sentences below.

1. The butterfly, which is a cousin to the moth, can be seen near flowerbeds during the day.
2. Butterflies, whose bodies are partly covered with multicolored scales, have six legs, four wings, and two antennae.
3. Because of many rows of scales, the butterfly has beautifully colored wings with fantastic designs.
4. The eye of a butterfly, which is made up of thousands of tiny lenses, sees color and movement very well.
5. The two antennae, which are located on the top of its head, are the smell sensors of the butterfly.
6. Because the butterfly is often in search of nectar, it flies from flower to flower.
7. While it searches for nectar, the butterfly performs an important job.
8. It carries pollen from one flower to another, which helps the flowers reproduce.
9. Butterfly caterpillars have mouth parts, which they use to chew leaves and other plant parts.
10. Because they damage crops, some kinds of caterpillars are considered pests.
11. Butterflies have a hard skin called the exoskeleton, which supports the body and protects the internal organs.
12. A butterfly that emits the appropriate scent during mating will be accepted immediately as a mate.

Name ______________________

A Day at Camp

A **complex sentence** contains one independent clause and one or more dependent clauses. The dependent clause may interrupt the independent clause, as in the second example below.

We look forward to going to camp every year because we have so much fun.

Our favorite camp, which is way up north, is open all summer long.

Draw a double line under the dependent clauses and a single line under the independent clauses.

6:45 A.M.	When the bugle plays at 6:45 A.M., all campers will rise.
7:00 A.M.	Because physical fitness is essential, a one-mile run is required.
7:30 A.M.	The showers, which are centrally located, will be available for use.
8:00 A.M.	Breakfast, which is always served promptly at 8:00 A.M., will be nutritious.
8:45 A.M.	Each camper is responsible for washing his own dishes because he will use them again at lunch.
9–11:30 A.M.	Morning activities, which include hiking, canoeing, and archery, will be open to everyone.
11:30–noon	Camper's awards will be presented to individuals when we gather for lunch.
Noon	Because everyone will be hungry, we will have a hearty lunch.
1:00–3:00 P.M.	Sign up for your favorite arts and crafts classes because space in each class is limited.
3:00–4:00 P.M.	We will swim each afternoon, whenever the weather cooperates.
5:00 P.M.	Camp cooks, who have prepared your evening meal, will dish it out at 5:00 P.M.
6:00 P.M.	When dinner is done, campers will be encouraged to perform skits.
7:00 P.M.	Scavenger hunts and games, which should be challenging, will begin.
8:00 P.M.	When there is no rain, we will sit around the campfire and sing songs.
9:00 P.M.	Because the bugle will blare early tomorrow, everyone must go to sleep.

Name ______________________________

Who Am I?

A **compound–complex sentence** contains two or more independent clauses and at least one dependent clause.

When you read the clues, you will begin to identify the mystery animal, and you will make your guess.

In these compound–complex sentences, underline the independent clauses once and the dependent clauses twice. Can you guess what animal this is?

1. Because the weather is turning cold, I will go south, and I will join others like myself.
2. I can weigh more than ten elephants, and when I am fully grown, my length is greater than a four-story building.
3. Scientists, who are called cetologists, know we have black and white markings, but that our markings differ from one another.
4. Though we all have similar markings, our individual ones are just as unique as a person's fingerprints, and they are as individual as a giraffe's spots.
5. I have a big tail, and I like to flip it up when I am traveling.
6. My skin, which covers my entire body, is smooth and hairless, but it is bumpy on parts of my head.
7. Although I eat huge amounts of food, I have no teeth, instead I have baleens.
8. If I rise out of the water, you might see my dorsal fins, or I might show you a glimpse of my tail.
9. Underneath my skin is a thick layer of dense fatty tissue, which is called blubber, and it maintains my body temperature at 93–99° F (34–37° C).
10. When I exhale, a jet of steam emerges from the top of my head, and it is released through a blowhole.
11. I communicate using a variety of moans and screams, and when I am mating, I use a special pattern of these, called "songs."

Name ______________________

Soup's On

A **simple sentence** contains one independent clause. A **compound sentence** is made of two independent clauses connected by a comma and conjunction. A **complex sentence** includes one independent clause and one or more dependent clauses. A **compound–complex sentence** contains two or more independent clauses (connected by a comma and conjunction) and at least one dependent clause.

> ***simple***: *I like soup.*
> ***compound***: *I like soup, and I prefer it hot.*
> ***complex***: *When I get home from school, I like soup.*
> ***compound-complex***: *When I get home from school, I like soup, and I prefer it hot.*

Identify the following sentences as **S** (simple), **C** (compound), **CX** (complex), or **C–CX** (compound–complex).

_____ 1. My grandma makes the best cheesy broccoli soup, and she serves it with homemade bread.

_____ 2. Big chunks of potatoes make potato soup worth eating.

_____ 3. Even though I hate pea soup, my mom always makes it.

_____ 4. Chili tastes great on a cold winter day.

_____ 5. Because we eat soup every Saturday night, we try lots of kinds, and we serve them in a variety of ways.

_____ 6. When we go out for Chinese food, we usually order egg drop soup.

_____ 7. In my opinion, a black bean soup with a rice and tomato salsa on top is the ultimate best.

_____ 8. If you come over tonight, you may stay for dinner, and we will share our minestrone.

_____ 9. Dad loves venison stew and whole wheat rolls.

_____ 10. Some people like clam chowder, but I'm not crazy about it.

_____ 11. When we're in a hurry, we just open a can of chicken noodle.

_____ 12. Kyle likes to eat at the Souper Bowl, where we go for soup and sandwiches, and he always orders their famous onion soup.

Name ______________________________

The Rodeo

A group of words punctuated like a sentence but not containing a complete thought is called a **fragment**. A fragment frequently lacks a subject or a predicate. Sometimes, a fragment may be corrected by adding a word or words. Other times, the correction is made by connecting the fragment to a preceding or following sentence and changing the punctuation.

fragment: *After the show.*
correct: *After the show, the audience exploded with applause.*

fragment: *One of the reasons I could not do my homework.*
correct: *One of the reasons I could not do my homework is that I went to the rodeo.*

Correct each of the fragments by connecting it to a "partner" sentence or group of words. Write the correct letter on the line. If the sentence is not a fragment, write **OK** on the line.

A. bareback riders use
B. entertain the crowd
C. untamed horses
D. great North American sport
E. doesn't use a saddle
F. bull riding
G. he gets bucked off
H. is thrilling

_____ 1. A bareback bronco rider.
_____ 2. For over 150 years, rodeo has been a.
_____ 3. At the rodeo, bucking broncos and their riders.
_____ 4. Riders mount in a stall called a chute.
_____ 5. A leather handle called a rigging to hang on to.
_____ 6. The eight second ride.
_____ 7. The cowboy tries to stay on the horse.
_____ 8. Will try to toss a rider off.
_____ 9. Then the pick-up man helps.
_____ 10. Is truly the most dangerous event.
_____ 11. If he can't hang on.
_____ 12. A clown distracts it.

Name ____________________

By the Shore

A **run-on sentence** consists of two or more complete sentences written without proper punctuation between them. Run-ons can be corrected in three ways.

1. If the two sentences are closely related, they can be separated by a semi-colon.

   Shells are very pretty; they make especially good necklaces.
2. Closely related sentences can also be separated with a comma and a conjunction.

   I like all kinds of fish, but angel fish are my favorite.
3. Sentences that are not closely related can be separated with a period.

   Puffer fish are funny-looking. They live in salt water.

Correct the run-ons below by adding the proper punctuation and conjunctions if necessary. If a sentence is not a run-on, write **OK** on the line.

_____ 1. The moray eel conceals himself by hiding in the rocks he pops his head out to catch his prey.

_____ 2. A group of sea animals named sea squirts shoot water through one of two body openings.

_____ 3. Starfish and sea urchins have no heads they have mouths on their bellies.

_____ 4. Starfish have five flexible arms they use them to walk around.

_____ 5. A seahorse is a fish that swims in an upright position the male has a kangaroo-like pouch that holds the fertilized eggs until they hatch.

_____ 6. Most sea urchins are vegetarians or scavengers most are equipped with five sharp teeth for scraping food.

_____ 7. Sand dollars are shallow-water echnioderms their bodies are covered with spines which aid in locomotion.

_____ 8. Seaweed is commonly found along rocky beaches because it grows attached to the rocks.

_____ 9. Female sea turtles come ashore to lay their eggs in holes, which they dig and then cover with sand.

_____ 10. A sea otter's hind feet are broadened into flippers his forefeet are useful for grasping.

_____ 11. The sea cucumber, a type of sea animal with a long, fleshy body, belongs to the echinoderm group.

_____ 12. Gulls are long-winged birds they are often seen flying and dipping over large bodies of water.

Name ______________________________

Monster Mile

Rewrite the article below, correcting the run-ons, fragments, and stringy sentences.

Seeker's Thrill amusement park has just released news that the world's most state-of-the-art roller coaster, the new Monster Mile, is ready to roll.

A select group of roller coaster enthusiasts will be the first to experience the ride since it is expected to be a sunny day at the park. The 100 special guests will strap-in at 9:00 A.M. and the ride will exceed record roller coaster speeds. Riders of the Monster Mile will stand during their 4.5 minute race through fifteen corkscrew loops, dozens of turns, and a mile of coaster track and the other roller coasters will not be running until the park opens. The park will be open to the public at 12:00 noon and the rides will run until 11:00 P.M., and parking will be free all day. Guests at Seeker's Thrill will be rewarded with a complimentary Monster Mile ice-cream bar after riding the thrilling roller coaster or some may choose not to ride the foreboding giant. Before leaving the park, however, anyone can purchase an "I survived the Monster Mile" t-shirt or hat then there will be a fireworks finale at 11:00 P.M. Seeker's Thrill will close at midnight on its grand opening day so have a great time and go "the Monster Mile!"

Name ______________________

In the Dohyo

Choppy sentences are a series of short, closely related sentences that, if joined together, could be made into one smoother and less repetitive sentence.

choppy sentences: *This book is interesting. It is a story about sumo wrestling. It is an exciting story.*

corrected sentence: *This book is an interesting and exciting story about sumo wrestling.*

Rewrite the choppy sentences below into smooth, non-repetitive sentences.

1. In Japan, sumo wrestlers are considered living icons. They are heroes of their national sport.
2. Sumo wrestlers prefer to be extremely large. Wrestlers strive to get very fat.
3. A tournament lasts for fifteen days. Wrestlers face a different opponent each day.
4. Wrestlers throw a handful of purifying salt. They must do this. They throw the salt before entering the hallowed ring.
5. The wrestling ring is considered a sacred place. It is called a *dohyo*.
6. Most matches are short. Most are intense. Most last less than one minute.
7. There is an important factor in sumo wrestling. Mental strength is important. It often provides the winning edge.
8. Slapping is allowed. Pushing is allowed. Tripping is allowed. Punching with the fist is not allowed.

comma use

Name ______________________________

After the Beep, Leave Your Message

A **comma** is used to set off an introductory phrase or dependent clause.
After a big day of sledding and skating, we made hot cocoa.

A **comma** is used after words of direct address at the beginning of a sentence.
Jodie, did you bring the marshmallows?

A **comma** is used after introductory words, such as, *yes, indeed, well, in addition to, thus,* and *moreover.*
Yes, I did.

Use two **commas** to set off interrupting words or expressions.
The marshmallows, I think, are a bit stale.

Place commas in the phone messages below.

- Hi call me when you get home. I will I think be home all evening.

- Greg I miss you. In addition to that I've got something exciting to tell you.

- Since you're not home yet I think I'll go shopping without you. By the way I did find your bracelet.

- Mom I went to Scott's. Yes I already did all of my English homework.

- Laura I received your request. For more information write to the Tennessee Tourist Association.

- Hello is this the Lewis residence? Your dog I believe is running loose on Jasper Court.

- Don't forget your dentist appointment Mr. Bean at 11:00 A.M. tomorrow morning. If you can't make it please call and cancel as soon as possible.

- This is Rebecca your niece calling at 5:00 P.M. If you still need a babysitter for Friday night I can do it.

Name ____________________

Prehistoric Creatures

Use **hyphens** to

a. break a word between syllables at the end of a line in running text.
b. join two-part numbers from twenty-one to ninety-nine.
c. write a fraction as a word.
d. join some compound nouns and adjectives.

a. Some scientists claim that dinosaurs roamed the earth mill-ions of years ago.
b. thirty-five, eighty-two
c. one-fortieth, two-thirds
d. fat-necked, hurricane-like

Add a hyphen to each of the following sentences. Then, in the blank, write the letter from above to show which rule you have applied.

_____ 1. The woolly mammoth was an elephant like animal covered with long, thick hair.

_____ 2. The mammoths had long, curved tusks useful during the winter in clear
ing away the snow to find grass to eat.

_____ 3. In permafrost regions of Siberia, some mammoths have been found per
fectly preserved.

_____ 4. The average Stegosaurus was twenty five feet long and weighed two to three tons.

_____ 5. The four sharp spikes on its tail were quite useful in wounding its ene
mies.

_____ 6. Triceratops, meaning "three horned face," was an aggressive dinosaur.

_____ 7. It chewed large amounts of plants with its razor sharp teeth.

_____ 8. Triceratops stood nine and one half feet tall.

_____ 9. Tyrannosaurus, a forty seven foot long tyrant, weighed seven tons.

_____ 10. Its huge jaws and sharp teeth helped make it the most pow
erful meat eater.

_____ 11. Brachiosaurus was an enormous herbivorous dino
saur.

_____ 12. It was seventy five feet long, forty feet tall, and weighed eighty tons.

Name ______________________________

Peter's Pizza

Quotation marks are used to enclose **direct quotation.** The end punctuation usually comes before the final quotation mark at the end of the quote. Always capitalize the first word of direct quotation. Do not capitalize the first word in the second part of an interrupted quotation unless the second part begins a new sentence.

Cameron said, "Would you like pizza for dinner?"

"Yes, that sounds good!" replied Angela. "I'll call Peter's and order one."

"After you order it," responded Cameron, "we will need to find some money."

Rewrite the following sentences by adding the correct punctuation and capitalization.

1. hello, this is Peter's Pizza how may I help you greeted Eric

____

____

2. i'd like a large pizza please Angela replied

____

3. What would you like on that Eric asked

____

4. I'll have pepperoni and anchovies said Angela

____

5. i'm sorry to tell you began Eric but we are out of pepperoni

____

____

6. oh, that's okay Angela responded i'll just have anchovies then

____

____

Continue Angela's conversation with Cameron when she gets off the phone. Write 4 more sentences with direct quotation.

1. ______________________________
2. ______________________________
3. ______________________________
4. ______________________________

Name ______________________________

Gossip

A **direct quotation** is the use of someone's exact words. It is always set off with quotation marks. An **indirect quotation** is the writer's description of someone else's words. It does not require quotation marks.

__direct__: Brent said, "Max is bringing the dog to the vet."
__indirect__: Brent said that Max is bringing the dog to the vet.

For each of the following sentences, write **DQ** (direct quotation) or **IQ** (indirect quotation) on the line. Then add quotation marks wherever they are needed.

The Orange Hair

____ 1. Jennifer asked, Did you see Rae's hair? It is bright orange!
____ 2. She dyed it herself! added Jordan.
____ 3. Yeah, sneered Tamara, she needs a wig.

The Surprise Party

____ 1. I'll see you at the party! declared Paige.
____ 2. What party? asked Maya.
____ 3. Steve's brothers are giving him a surprise birthday party, answered Paige, and everyone is going.
____ 4. Maya said that she would love to go, too.

The Joke

____ 1. Don't look now, warned Jeff, but Robby is about to drink his pop.
____ 2. So what? Anna questioned.
____ 3. Dan told Anna about the plastic worm that they had dropped in Robby's cup.
____ 4. Jeff then said that Robby had just spit his pop across the table.

The Romance

____ 1. Sarah mentioned that Rachelle was crazy about Emilio.
____ 2. No way! interjected Kate. He's such a creep!
____ 3. Maybe, but he's gorgeous, reminded Allison.
____ 4. Too bad, added Tamara, because he likes Stacey Pool.

colon

Name ______________________________

In the Pool!

A **colon** is used between the hour and the minutes when time is written using numbers. A **colon** is also used to introduce a list or a series of things unless the series is preceded by an expression, such as, *for example, namely, for instance,* or *that is.*

School begins at 8:20 A.M. each day, Monday through Friday.

I have to take several things to school each day: my backpack, my lunch, and my house key.

I have to take several things to school each day, ***namely****, my backpack, my lunch, and my house key.* (no colon necessary)

Write the time correctly in the blanks using numbers and colons.

__________ My swimming class begins at nine thirty A.M. each morning.

__________ We change into our suits and quickly shower by nine thirty-five.

__________ If we're not sitting on the bench at the exact time, we will have five extra laps during our warm-up, which lasts for ten minutes.

__________ Then, we practice our strokes until five after ten.

__________ Next, we do rescue drills for ten minutes.

__________ Diving practice follows until ten twenty-five.

__________ Then we have just five minutes to shower and change back into our clothes.

__________ Can you believe we have to be back to our next class by ten forty A.M.?

Punctuate these lists correctly.

1. There are several categories of swimmers beginner intermediate and advanced.
2. Many of my classmates are excellent divers namely Pete Carlos Susan Amanda and Yong.
3. Every day I take a bag of items to class swimsuit shampoo hairbrush and deodorant.
4. Today we practiced some strokes for example the breaststroke backstroke and butterfly.
5. In the locker room, there is a huge pile of towels of all colors green blue red orange and purple.
6. After swimming, I still have four more classes that include Algebra English General Science and Band.

Name ______________________

The History of the World

> A **semicolon** is used to join two independent clauses that are closely related if a conjunction is not used. (An **independent clause** is a group of words that could stand as a complete sentence by itself.)
>
> *The Olympic Games originated in ancient Greece; Greek gods were important to the people of Greece.*
> (incorrect, these sentences are not closely related.)
>
> *The Olympic Games originated in ancient Greece; the main event was the pentathlon.*
> (correct, these sentences are closely related.)

Determine whether the following sentences are joined correctly. Write **Yes** on the line if they are; write **No** if they are not.

_____ 1. The Phoenicians were the most famous traders of the ancient world; they traded papyrus, ivory, glass, and wool.

_____ 2. The Persians built roads and canals; Alexander the Great's army defeated them.

_____ 3. Hittite rulers signed some of the first treaties; treaties helped to bring about peace.

_____ 4. Egyptian writing was based in hieroglyphics; the Egyptians worshipped many gods.

_____ 5. Ancient Greece was divided into city-states; Athens and Sparta were rivals.

_____ 6. Roman citizens were separated into two classes; the plebeians were commoners, and the patricians were nobles.

_____ 7. Charlemange was a great ruler and warrior during medieval times; his kingdom extended over most of western Europe.

_____ 8. King John became king of England in 1199; he signed the Magna Carta.

_____ 9. During the Renaissance, Leonardo daVinci painted the *Mona Lisa* and *The Last Supper*; he is considered an artistic genius.

_____ 10. The Protestant Reformation was a religious revolt against the Roman Catholic Church; Martin Luther was a German clergyman.

_____ 11. Napoleon Bonaparte created a French empire after the revolution; he ruled as a military dictator.

_____ 12. The Industrial Revolution followed the Enlightenment; it was a time when power-driven machinery began to replace manual labor.

_____ 13. World War I started in 1914; it was considered the war to end all wars.

_____ 14. A world-wide depression occurred in the 1930s; many people lost their jobs and their homes.

Answer Key

Working Words

Many words act as various parts of speech depending on their use in a sentence.

work
*I really enjoy my **work**.* (noun)
*Mr. James assembled the **work** force.* (adjective)
*Most people **work** hard to earn a living.* (verb)

Identify the part of speech of each boldfaced word: N (noun), V (verb), ADJ (adjective), or ADV (adverb).

N 1. Read a **book** just for fun.
V 2. It's important to **book** your reservations well in advance.
ADJ 3. The **book** cover protects the old classic.

V 4. **Duck** before you get hit!
ADJ 5. He used a **duck** call to attract the flying fowl.
N 6. **Ducks** rest in the reeds by the pond.

ADJ 7. Living in the country, we drink **well** water.
N 8. Our **well** has never run dry.
ADV 9. Drink lots of water, and you will feel **well**.

ADJ 10. That was a **wrong** turn in the opposite direction.
N 11. Can you learn to overlook a **wrong**?
V 12. She had been **wronged**.

N 13. The clouds are heavy with rain.
V 14. It **rained** cats and dogs all day long.
ADJ 15. The **rain** forests are very important natural resources.

Using the parts of speech given, write sentences for the word **trick**.

(noun) 1. Answers will vary.
(adjective) 2. ____
(verb) 3. ____

Page 4

Hanukkah

noun—person, place, or thing
adjective—modifies a noun
preposition—relates a noun or pronoun to another
conjunction—links two or more words or groups of words
verb—shows action or a state of being
adverb—modifies a verb
article—a, an, the (modify nouns)
pronoun—can be singular, plural, or possessive; takes the place of a noun
interjection—a word or phrase used in exclamation to express emotion

Read the narrative below and determine the part of speech of the word that follows each number. Write the part of speech from the box above on the corresponding line below.

My family observes Hanukkah, an 1. important holiday celebrated by the Jewish people. It 2. begins each year on the twenty-fifth day of the Hebrew month of Kislev 3. and lasts eight days. 4. Hanukkah usually falls 5. in December.

Hanukkah 6. is called the Feast of Lights. One important symbol of the 7. holiday is the *menorah*. A menorah is a candlestick with 8. nine cups for candles. The ninth cup holds the *shamash* 9. candle. Each night of Hanukkah 10. my father lights the shamash candle 11. first and uses it 12. to light the other candles. One candle is lit 13. each night 14. until the final night of Hanukkah.

Hanukkah is 15. a time of gift giving and game playing too. The children 16. receive gifts and sing songs. 17. Wow, can you believe we children sometimes get money during Hanukkah? One of my favorite things to do is play with the dreidel, which is used to play games during the 18. holiday. The dreidel is a 19. toplike toy with a Hebrew letter 20. inscribed on each side.

During Hanukkah, we 21. joyously celebrate the history of our people and our religion.

1. adjective
2. verb
3. conjunction
4. noun
5. preposition
6. verb
7. noun
8. adjective
9. noun
10. pronoun
11. adverb
12. verb
13. adjective
14. preposition
15. article
16. verb
17. interjection
18. noun
19. adjective
20. verb
21. adverb

Page 5

Yikes!

An **interjection** is a word that is used alone to express strong emotions.

Wow!, Oh!, Whew!, Hey!

Supply an interjection for each of the comics below.

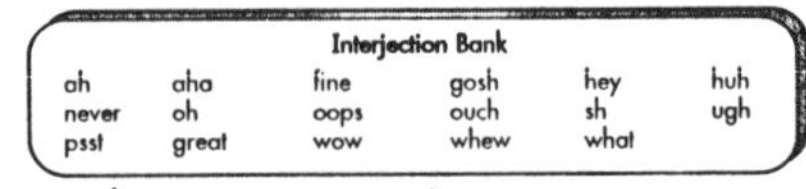

Interjection Bank

ah	aha	fine	gosh	hey	huh
never	oh	oops	ouch	sh	ugh
psst	great	wow	whew	what	

Answers will vary.

____! Bring that back!
____! That's gross!
____! Did I do that?

____! Look out below!
____! Over here fella.

____! Lifting weights is for whimps.
____! Look at that!

Page 6

Crispy Critters

A **conjunction** is a word that is used to join words or groups of words.

*Dogs **and** wolves howl.*
*I'm happy, **for** today I bought a kitten.*

Write a conjunction in each of the blanks below to complete the Crispy Critters advertisement. Use each conjunction once, but use *and* three times.

Conjunction Bank

neither	nor	either	or	and	not only
but also	while	so	for	yet	

Some cats are treated like pets, while others are treated like family. Show your favorite feline that you love and respect him by bringing home CRISPY CRITTERS kitty food! CRISPY CRITTERS will not only make your cat happier, but also more energetic and lively. CRISPY CRITTERS comes in four tasty flavors, so choose his favorite. Select either chicken, beef, or seafood. Other cat foods claim to satisfy most cats, yet don't back their claims with research. You can be sure that when you buy CRISPY CRITTERS you will neither waste money nor disappoint your feline friends. CRISPY CRITTERS is delicious and nutritious and a hit every time. Buy CRISPY CRITTERS today, for every day your cat will thank you!

Crispy Critters

Page 7

Let's Get Together

Contractions tie two words together to make a new word. An apostrophe takes the place of the letters that have been removed.

let + us = let's
that + would = that'd

Write the two small words in each equation that have been put together to make each contraction.

can't = can + not		aren't = are + not	
don't = do + not		doesn't = does + not	
isn't = is + not		hasn't = has + not	
mustn't = must + not		haven't = have + not	
won't = will + not		hadn't = had + not	
shouldn't = should + not		needn't = need + not	
couldn't = could + not		weren't = were + not	
didn't = did + not		mightn't = might + not	

Combine each set of words below to make more contractions.

1. I am	I'm	7. we are	we're
2. he will	he'll	8. we will	we'll
3. it is	it's	9. you are	you're
4. they had	they'd	10. that is	that's
5. could have	could've	11. she had	she'd
6. I had	I'd	12. they have	they've

Page 8

At the Front

A **prefix** is one or more syllables added to the beginning of a word to form a new word.

un + believer = unbeliever
mis + trust = mistrust
off + shoot = offshoot

Match a prefix with a root word to form a new word.

Answer	Prefix	Root
G	1. anti	A. merge
J	2. tele	B. claim
A	3. sub	C. call
F	4. under	D. live
B	5. pro	E. ordinary
H	6. en	F. cover
C	7. re	G. freeze
D	8. out	H. courage
E	9. extra	I. meter
I	10. peri	J. phone

Answer	Prefix	Root
J	1. post	A. eager
E	2. bi	B. tanker
H	3. co	C. organized
I	4. mini	D. clockwise
A	5. over	E. cycle
F	6. extra	F. fine
B	7. super	G. violent
G	8. non	H. author
C	9. ultra	I. skirt
D	10. counter	J. war

Select words from above and use them to write five sentences.

1. Answers will vary.
2.
3.
4.
5.

Page 9

Bring Up the Rear

A **suffix** is one or more syllables added to the end of a word to form a new word.

love + able = lovable
motion + less = motionless

Complete the classified ads by adding suffixes to the words that are followed by a blank line.

-ing -dom -able -ment -ship -ade -ure -ful -ness -ance

The School Times — **Classified** — May 2000

Help Wanted

ARE YOU SUFFERing from boredom? You can have a pleasur(e)able summer working at the ThunderCaverns Amusement Park. For information, call 1-800-FUN-SOAK.

Meetings

Your attendance is welcome at the town meeting. We will discuss issues of freedom and citizenship.

Demand fairness and good treatment for your pigs. They are pets too! Come and speak about your concerns for our lov(e)able swine.

70s Party

WEAR YOUR BELL BOTTOM JEANS and peace-sign jewelry to make a groovy statement at this retro bash. The DJ will be playing danc(e)ing music all night long.

For Sale

FRESH AND DELICIOUS lemonade and butter cookies with lemon ic(e)ing made by the varsity cheerleaders.

South City's soccer team is selling chocolate bars. Buy several and enjoy the sweetness!

Tutoring

DOES ALGEBRA HAVE YOU feeling like a failure? Sign up for tutoring. It's helpful and fun. Call Mr. X for info.

FINISH HIGH SCHOOL and begin your adult life with wis(e)dom! A diploma puts you on the path to a successful life.

VOTE! VOTE! VOTE!

Everyone's vote is useful in determin(e)ing our class officers. Show your class spirit and *VOTE TODAY!*

An announcement will be made on Monday to congratulate the winners for school government.

BIG MUSIC TRADE

Trade your CDs at the Music Kingdom on Saturday at 10:00 A.M. It will be more profitable than painful. Plus, there will be live entertainment and good refreshment.

Reading the classifieds is good expos(e)ure to the town's happenings.

Page 10

The Short of It

Use **abbreviations** with other words or names; never use them by themselves. Avoid using abbreviations in running text. It is more proper to spell out abbreviated words when they appear in a sentence. Capitalize the abbreviations of proper nouns.

I live at 1315 Trail ct., Madison, oh 21461. (incorrect)
My address: 1315 Trail Ct., Madison, OH 21461 (correct)
Christmas is in Dec. (incorrect)
Dec. 25th, 2002 (correct)

Match each noun to its abbreviation.

Answer	Noun	Answer	Noun		
F	1. apartment	C	7. Incorporated	A. Rd.	G. pp.
H	2. volume	K	8. Company	B. cont.	H. vol.
A	3. Road	B	9. continued	C. Inc.	I. misc.
E	4. Reverend	D	10. Corporation	D. Corp.	J. lat.
I	5. miscellaneous	L	11. anonymous	E. Rev.	K. Co.
J	6. latitude	G	12. pages	F. apt.	L. anon.

In the blanks, write C if the abbreviation was used correctly; write N if it was not.

N 1. We live in an apt.
C 2. Apt. 303, Sudsby Rd.
C 3. Rev. Martin
N 4. My father works for a big corp.
N 5. For homework, we were assigned pp. 94–115 in *Great Expectations*.
N 6. I hate to watch a show that will be cont. the next day.
N 7. Please turn down the vol.
N 8. We used money from the misc. category of our budget to buy the gift.
C 9. Timber Lumber Co.
N 10. Their co. cont. to grow.
C 11. Extras and misc.
N 12. Our lesson will be cont. tomorrow.

Page 11

It's Important!

Capitalize the names of books, movies, plays, songs, poems, television programs, and works of art. Also capitalize the names and titles of people.

Little Women
General Schwartzkopf

Rewrite the following titles using capitals correctly.

Movie:	*a bug's life*	A Bug's Life
Poem:	"the road not taken"	"The Road Not Taken"
Play:	*romeo and juliet*	Romeo and Juliet
T.V. Show:	"the simpsons"	"The Simpsons"
Art Work:	*the starry night*	The Starry Night
Song:	"the star spangled banner"	"The Star Spangled Banner"
Book:	*roll of thunder, hear my cry*	Roll of Thunder, Hear My Cry

Write your favorite titles using capitals correctly.

Movie: Answers will vary.
Poem:
Play:
T.V. Show:
Art Work:
Song:
Book:

Put an X on the line if the title is written correctly. If it is not, write the title correctly on the line that follows.

__ the spice Girls The Spice Girls
X Vice President Gerald R. Ford
__ Where In The World Is Carmen San Diego? Where in the World Is Carmen San Diego?
X Dr. Sigmund Freud
__ how many feet in the bed? How Many Feet in the Bed?
__ the Polar Express The Polar Express

Page 12

To Whom It May Concern:

Every business letter must have the following:
heading—your name and full address
inside address—the name, title, company, and address of the recipient
date—write out the date in words (e.g., September 14, 1999).
salutation—a formal greeting, "Dear Mr. Buckle,"
body—a concise message written in paragraph form; leave a space between paragraphs.
closing—a formal closing, "Sincerely,"
signature—leave 4 spaces and print your full name; write your signature above it.

Write a business letter to Mr. Fashion, clothing designer of Lookin' Good Fashions Corporation, 500 Style Street, New York City, NY 21112. Suggest your fashion ideas for people your age and request a fashion adjustment that would benefit you personally.

Heading: Answers will vary.

Inside Address: Mr. Fashion, clothing designer
Lookin' Good Fashions Corporation
500 Style Street
New York City, NY 21112

Date:

Salutation: Dear Mr. Fashion,
Body:

Closing: Sincerely,
Signature:
Full Name:

Page 13

Louisa May Alcott

A **proper noun** is the name of a particular person, place, or thing. Proper nouns are always capitalized. All other nouns are called **common nouns**. Common nouns are not usually capitalized and refer only to general people, places, or things.

proper nouns: *Joseph, England, Vermont, Pepsi*
common nouns: *boy, country, state, beverage*

Underline all the nouns (both common and proper) in the sentences below.

1. Louisa May Alcott is remembered as a great American author.
2. She was born in Germantown, Pennsylvania, on November 29, 1832.
3. She considered Ralph Waldo Emerson and Henry David Thoreau her friends.
4. Louisa grew up in a poor family in New England where she made and sold dolls' clothes to earn money.
5. When she was a little older, she taught school and began writing.
6. In 1854, Miss Alcott published her first book entitled *Flower Fables*.
7. Several of her stories were published in *Atlantic Monthly*.
8. Eventually, she wrote *Little Women*, a semi-autobiographical novel.
9. Other books based on Alcott's life include *Little Men* and *Jo's Boys*.
10. Today, readers can enjoy her biography, *Invincible Louisa*, written by Cornelia Meigs.

Write the nouns from the sentences in the correct category below.

Common Nouns		Proper Nouns	
author	stories	Louisa May Alcott	Miss Alcott
friends	novel	Germantown	Flower Fables
family	books	Pennsylvania	Atlantic Monthly
clothes	life	November	Litte Women
money	readers	R.W. Emerson	Litte Men
school	biography	H.D. Thoreau	Jo's Boys
book		Louisa	Invincible Louisa
		New England	Cornelia Meigs

Page 14

Patches on Jackets and Dresses

Plural nouns represent more than one.

According to the rule given, write the plural form of each of the following words. In each, the first two have been done as examples.

To form the plural of most nouns, just add *s*. If the noun ends in *s, x, ch, sh, z,* or *ss*, add *es*.

1. (jacket) *jackets*	5. (dress) *dresses*	9. (patch) patches
2. (shirt) shirts	6. (sash) sashes	10. (fax) faxes
3. (sock) socks	7. (swatch) swatches	11. (tie) ties
4. (buzz) buzzes	8. (belt) belts	12. (jean) jeans

For nouns that end in *y* preceded by a vowel, just add *s*. For nouns that end in *y* preceded by a consonant, change the *y* to *i* and add *es*.

1. (boy) *boys*	5. (treaty) *treaties*	9. (family) families
2. (tray) trays	6. (ploy) ploys	10. (tragedy) tragedies
3. (spray) sprays	7. (mystery) mysteries	11. (salary) salaries
4. (baby) babies	8. (malady) maladies	12. (candy) candies

To form the plural of a word that ends in an *o* preceded by a vowel, add *s*. For words that end in an *o* preceded by a consonant, usually add *es*. (There may be some exceptions to this rule.)

1. (tomato) *tomatoes*	5. (zoo) *zoos*	9. (potato) potatoes
2. (avocado) avocados	6. (hero) heroes	10. (dingo) dingoes
3. (buffalo) buffaloes	7. (stereo) stereos	11. (kangaroo) kangaroos
4. (zero) zeros	8. (rodeo) rodeos	12. (duo) duos

For words that end in *f* or *fe*, change the *f* to *v* and add *es*; some of these words simply add *s*. (You may need to consult a dictionary to be certain.)

1. (scarf) *scarves*	5. (chief) *chiefs*	9. (thief) thieves
2. (knife) knives	6. (shelf) shelves	10. (half) halves
3. (leaf) leaves	7. (elf) elves	11. (belief) beliefs
4. (motif) motifs	8. (life) lives	12. (loaf) loaves

Page 15

Concrete or Asphalt?

An **abstract noun** names an idea, quality, or state of mind. It is something not perceivable through any of the five senses.
A **concrete noun** names something that can be seen or touched.

abstract nouns: *peace, patience, success, sadness*
concrete nouns: *road, flower, house, animal, Joe*

Circle the concrete nouns. Underline the abstract nouns.

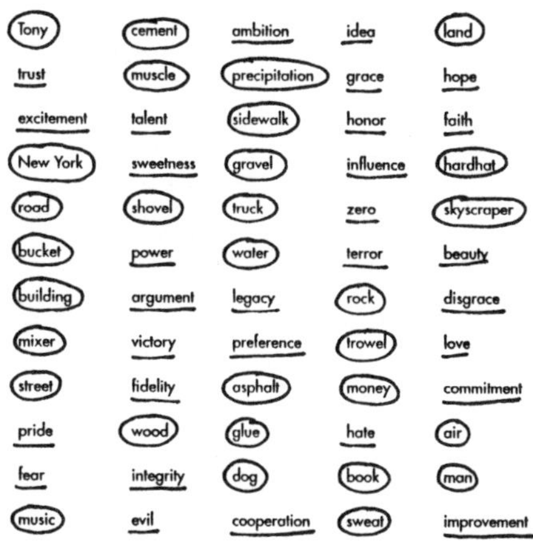

Tony	cement	ambition	idea	land
trust	muscle	precipitation	grace	hope
excitement	talent	sidewalk	honor	faith
New York	sweetness	gravel	influence	hardhat
road	shovel	truck	zero	skyscraper
bucket	power	water	terror	beauty
building	argument	legacy	rock	disgrace
mixer	victory	preference	trowel	love
street	fidelity	asphalt	money	commitment
pride	wood	glue	hate	air
fear	integrity	dog	book	man
music	evil	cooperation	sweat	improvement

Page 16

Boy or Girl?

Gender of nouns refers to the sex indicated by the noun.
The four genders are
masculine—male
feminine—female
neuter—no sex
indefinite—could be either male or female

masculine: *knight, prince*
feminine: *aunt, empress*
neuter: *chair, car*
indefinite: *nurse, teacher*

Write the following words under the correct category.

baby	flower	sister	queen	neighbor	rocket
nephew	shoe	husband	principal	mother	uncle
damsel	grandpa	lunch	prince	book	niece
pool	friend	lad	seamstress	princess	teacher
son	table	actor	nurse		

MASCULINE	FEMININE	NEUTER	INDEFINITE
nephew	damsel	pool	baby
son	sister	flower	friend
grandpa	queen	shoe	principal
husband	seamstress	table	nurse
lad	mother	lunch	neighbor
uncle	princess	book	teacher
prince	niece	rocket	actor

Page 17

Marching Pride

Nouns that show ownership are called **possessive nouns**. To form the possessive of a singular noun add **'s**. To form a plural possessive add **s'**. If the noun is already in the plural form and ends in an *s*, simply add an apostrophe. If the plural form does not end in an *s*, add **'s**.

singular possessive noun: *Cindy's chair, dog's bone, piano's keys*
plural possessive noun: *ladies' purses, houses' windows, children's lunches, women's club*

Rewrite the phrases by using possessive nouns.

1. Drumsticks belonging to drummers drummers' drumsticks
2. The reed of the clarinet clarinet's reed
3. Baton belonging to the drum major drum major's baton
4. Instruments of the musicians musicians' instruments
5. Sound of the tubas tubas' sound
6. Colorful flags of the color guard color guard's colorful flags
7. Slide belonging to the trombone trombone's slide
8. Crash made by cymbals cymbals' crash
9. New uniforms owned by the band band's new uniforms
10. Cases for instruments instruments' cases
11. Spats for the shoes shoes' spats
12. Solo of the saxophone saxophone's solo

Add apostrophes to the possessive nouns in the paragraph below.

The band's members march in perfect unison onto the football field. The players' hearts beat wildly as the adrenaline pumps throughout their bodies. At the drum major's cue, the musicians lift their instruments. Music and movement explode together in a powerful show for the audience's pleasure. Judges' scores are recorded as the band performs. The spectators' appreciation is shown with a standing ovation. The band's pride can be felt as they bow before the crowd. At the end of the competition, the bands all stand at attention awaiting the announcement of the final placements and the awarding of their group's trophy.

Page 18

All Together!

A **collective noun** names a group of people, places, or things. When a collective noun refers to a group as a unit, it is considered singular. When it refers to the individual members of the group who are acting separately, it is considered plural.

singular collective nouns:
*The **school** of fish live in the cool water.*
*Our **team** usually wins.*

plural collective nouns:
*The **school** of fish are all swimming in different directions to avoid the predator.*
*The **team** are all expected to earn good grades in school.*

Match the collective nouns.

F	1. colony	A. cotton
B	2. fleet	B. ships
G	3. squad	C. lies
J	4. grove	D. geese
A	5. bale	E. diamonds
D	6. gaggle	F. ants
C	7. pack	G. police
I	8. nest	H. cards
E	9. cluster	I. snakes
H	10. deck	J. trees

Mark the following sentences S (singular) or P (plural). Circle the correct verb.

P 1. The family (is, **are**) all opening their gifts together.
S 2. Grandma's batch of cookies (**is**, are) baking in the oven.
S 3. Mom's set of Christmas china (**is**, are) waiting on the table.
P 4. The cleaning staff (is, **are**) not working today; they are home with their families.
S 5. The company (**is**, are) due to arrive soon.

Write 4 sentences using the indicated collective nouns. You choose whether to make them singular or plural.

(class) 1. Answers will vary.
(crowd) 2.
(herd) 3.
(tribe) 4.

Page 19

Cold-Blooded

A **predicate noun** is a noun used as a subject complement (the subject of the sentence and the predicate noun represent the same thing). Predicate nouns follow linking verbs.

Leo was the fiercest lion in the zoo.
Leo = lion

In each of the following sentences, circle the simple subject and underline the simple predicate noun. Then complete the equation.

1. Reptiles are a specific group of animals. reptiles - group
2. They are creatures that are cold-blooded. they - creatures
3. A snake is a reptile. snake - reptile
4. The swamp is home to many snakes. swamp - home
5. Iguanas are also members of the reptile family. iguanas - members
6. They are lizards that have spines from head to toe. they - lizards
7. The desert is a good habitat for a wide variety of snakes and lizards. desert - habitat
8. The huge dinosaurs that once roamed the earth were reptiles. dinosaurs - reptiles
9. Tyrannosaurus was a flesh-eating dinosaur that lived on land. Tyrannosaurus - dinosaur
10. Crocodiles and alligators are dangerous reptilian hunters. Crocodiles and alligators - hunters
11. The turtle's shell is his home. shell - home
12. Some people think snakes, lizards, and turtles are good pets. snakes, lizards, and turtles - pets
13. Frogs are amphibians and do not belong to the reptile family. frogs - amphibians
14. Some reptiles are egg layers. reptiles - layers
15. The python is a constricting snake. python - snake

Page 20

Dear Santa

Pronouns are words that take the place of nouns. A **personal pronoun** indicates the speaker (first person), the one spoken to (second person), or the one spoken about (third person).

first-person pronouns: *I, my, mine, me, we, our, ours, us*
second-person pronouns: *you, your, yours*
third-person pronouns: *he, she, it, his, hers, its, him, her, they, their, theirs, them*

In the parentheses next to each personal pronoun, indicate whether the pronoun is first (1), second (2), or third (3) person.

Dear Santa,

I (1) haven't believed in you (2) since I (1) was seven years old, but for many years my (1) parents shamelessly participated in the scam to deceive me (1) about your (2) existence. Year after year they (3) took me (1) to see you (2) at the mall. Tales of your (2) home in the North Pole and of your (2) elves further supported their (3) story. Of course, each Christmas morning I (1) received several gifts from you (2). But, the fact is, it (3) just didn't make sense. How could you (2) travel around the entire world in just one night, deliver millions of gifts, and eat literally tons of cookies? Impossible, I (1) say!

This isn't just about me, (1) either. My (1) little sister still believes in you, and I (1) am concerned about her (3). Is it (3) good to lie to a little girl? She (3), like many other trusting children, will one day learn the truth. They (3) will be heartbroken; their (3) dreams will be shattered. Santa, how can you (2) traumatize them (3) like this? I (1) urge you (2) to come clean and tell them (3) the truth, sir.

Sincerely,
Jeremy

P.S. In case you (2) are coming to our (1) house this Christmas Eve, I (1) could use a new stereo.

Page 21

Colorful Clues

When a pronoun is the subject of the sentence, it is called a **subject pronoun**. When a pronoun is used as the direct object, indirect object, or object of the preposition, it is called an **object pronoun**. A pronoun must agree with its antecedent in both number and gender.

She dropped the book. (subject)
Eric picked it up. (direct object)
Betsy gave him a big smile. (indirect object)
Eric would do anything for her. (object of the preposition)

Underline the pronoun in each sentence. On the line, write S if the pronoun is a subject; write O if the pronoun is an object.

O 1. Elephants wear it.
S 2. It is as dark as the darkest night.
O 3. Grandma gave us slippers which perfectly match the delicate hue on the inside of a rabbit's ear.
S 4. I bought a chocolate-colored sweater when I was shopping at the mall.
S 5. He has eyes that sparkle like beautiful ocean water.
S 6. I am the acronym for all of the colors of the rainbow.
O 7. The shirt that looks like electric sunshine belongs to him.
O 8. Kathryn described to her the cat's fur, which was like fluffy clouds on a sunny day.
S 9. We are thinking about painting the exterior of the house the color of pumpkin.
O 10. Larry told me that Joe prefers the color of money.
O 11. Grapes that had been dipped in nature's royal paint appeared all around him.
O 12. Apples, cherries, and some fast cars are dressed in it.

Fill in an appropriate pronoun to take the place of each noun followed by a line. Write the pronoun on the line.

1. Alan and Dutch think the house *it* is the best color of all.
2. I gave my red shoes to Meredith *her*.
3. David picked up Lucy *her* in an orange convertible.
4. Laura gave Michael *him* a juicy piece of pink watermelon.
5. Shelby bought a pink teddy bear for her baby sister *her*.
6. Renee *She* dropped the pot of hot, red tomato sauce.

Page 22

Shoes Galore

An **antecedent** is the noun to which a pronoun refers. The antecedent may be in the same sentence as the pronoun, or it may appear in another sentence nearby.

*The guys shined their shoes after **they** finished walking through the mud.* (they refers to guys)

Read the paragraph below. Draw an arrow from each italicized pronoun to its antecedent. Then complete the chart below for each pronoun-antecedent pair you found.

My family has a large shoe closet in *our* vestibule. *It* is a mess because everyone just kicks *their* shoes inside. If you would dig through that pile you would find many different kinds of footwear in *it*; my brother's cleats, Mom's three-inch high heels, and Dad's dirty work boots are among *them*. My sister Maggie has about a hundred pair of shoes. *She* has red cowboy boots, summer sandals, weird looking clogs, and running shoes, just to name a few. *They* are all in the heap. The pile is growing bigger, and *it* is a pain in the neck. Finding a matching pair in that mess takes forever. Someone needs to clean *it* up. I think I'll tell my sister that *she* has to do it!

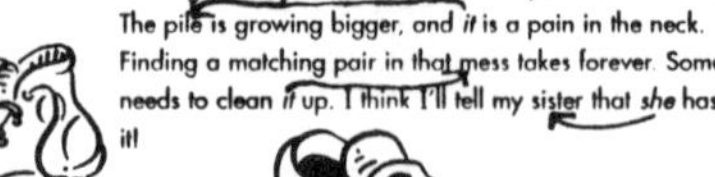

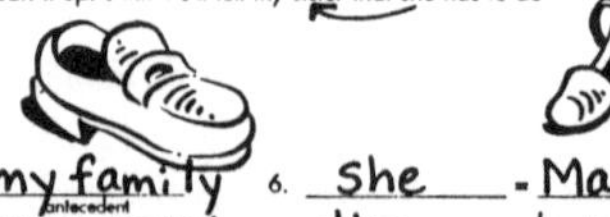

	pronoun		antecedent		pronoun		antecedent
1.	our	-	my family	6.	she	-	Maggie
2.	it	-	shoe closet	7.	they	-	boots, sandals...
3.	their	-	everyone	8.	it	-	pile
4.	it	-	pile	9.	it	-	mess
5.	them	-	footwear	10.	she	-	sister

Page 23

Piranha and Porpoises

A **pronoun** must agree with its antecedent in number and gender.
Madeline is my cousin, and she lives nearby. (feminine, singular)
Eric and Tim, are my cousins, and they live nearby too. (masculine, plural)
Aunt Trudy has a truck, and it is red. (neuter, singular)

Circle all of the pronouns in the journal entry below. Write an F over all feminine pronouns, an M over all masculine pronouns, an I over all indefinite pronouns, and an N over all neuter pronouns. Also, write an S if it is singular or a P if it is plural. The first one is done for you.

You (I-S) won't believe how much fun I (I-S) had! Last week my (I-S) class went to Chicago to visit the Shedd Aquarium. Mrs. Drake split us (I-P) into six groups, and we (I-P) all went different directions. My (I-S) group toured the aquarium cases first. There were all sorts of fish from different parts of the world. The best fish were the South American ones. My (I-S) friend, Mary, didn't like the piranha. She (F-S) thought they (N-P) were creepy. I (I-S) loved them (N-P).

Next we (I-P) went to see the dolphin show. An aquarium worker came out and stood on rocks in the water. He (M-S) used whistles and hand signals to make the dolphins jump, swim backwards, and talk. It (N-S) was really amazing!

Our (I-P) next stop was in the basement, where we (I-P) saw the beluga whales. They (N-P) were the color of snow and played with each other, swimming side by side. We (I-P) also saw penguins in the basement. Eric and Matt were really mean; they (M-P) banged on the glass to scare the penguins.

We (I-P) were allowed only ten minutes in the gift shop, so I (I-S) only bought a dolphin key chain for my (I-S) brother. He (M-S) loves dolphins.

We (I-P) had a great time, and I (I-S) can't wait to see it (N-S) all over again.

Page 24

Sports Fanatics

An **indefinite pronoun** is one that refers generally, not specifically, to people, places, or things. Some indefinite pronouns are always singular, some are always plural, and some may be either singular or plural.
singular indefinite pronouns: *anybody, anyone, another, each, either, everybody, everyone, nobody, no one, neither, one, other, someone, somebody, everything, anything, something*
plural indefinite pronouns: *many, both, few, several, others*
singular or plural indefinite pronouns: *all, any, most, some, none*

In each of the following sentences, underline the indefinite pronouns. Circle the verb that agrees in number with the indefinite pronoun acting as the subject.

1. Everyone in my family (love, **loves**) to watch football on Sunday afternoons.
2. Several of my friends and I (**play**, plays) baseball.
3. After school, some of the guys (**practice**, practices) basketball on our street.
4. In our little town, no one (know, **knows**) much about ice hockey.
5. Many (**choose**, chooses) tennis while others (prefer, prefers) racquetball.
6. All of the schools in our community (has, **have**) soccer teams.
7. Does anyone (**consider**, considers) pool a sport?
8. Someone in our class (claim, **claims**) table tennis is an Olympic sport.
9. In the ring, both boxers (**take**, takes) a beating.
10. Each speed skater (race, **races**) against the clock to get the best time possible.
11. Fortunately, somebody (**was able**, were able) to get us tickets to the ice-skating competition.
12. Either of them could (**participate**, participates) in the track and field finals.
13. Few of my friends (**dive**, dives) well.
14. I think everything about sumo wrestling (**is**, are) totally cool.
15. Nobody (call, **calls**) chess a sport. Right?

Page 25

Peanuts

A **possessive pronoun** is one which indicates ownership or possession. Possessive pronouns include: **my, mine, your, yours, his, her, hers, its, our, ours, their, theirs.**
*He forgot **his** peanuts as he raced out of school.*

Read the story, underline all of the pronouns, and circle all of the possessive pronouns.

Lou loved peanuts. Lou's mom bought huge amounts of peanuts to keep him satisfied. But, despite her attempts, her son's ravenous appetite for peanuts grew with each passing day. Lou carried them in his pockets, which bulged like satchels at his waist. Everywhere we went he shucked his peanuts, leaving a crunchy trail of shells behind him. The problem increased until our gym teacher finally refused to let him play volleyball after all the players began slipping on his shellings. Our teammates lost their patience, too, and suggested Lou sit out. He protested, but our team just yelled, "You're through, Lou!"

Then, on Saturday, Lou met his terrible fate. While enjoying a riveting performance at the circus and munching feverishly on his favorite snack, my friend Lou was attacked by a hungry baby elephant. She apparently broke free when she smelled Lou's pocketful of peanuts. She thought the peanuts should be hers! And so, Lou's peanut-eating days are at an end. It pains me to report the conclusion of this tale about a dear friend of mine.

Poor Lou, we will miss you.

Page 26

Who? What?

An **interrogative pronoun** introduces a question. Interrogative pronouns include: **who, whom, whose, what,** and **which.**
Who is at the door?
What does he want?

Underline the interrogative pronouns in the sentences below.

A Good Movie
1. With whom did you see the movie?
2. Whose ticket stub is this?
3. What did you think of the special effects?
4. Which actor was your favorite?
5. Who do you think would enjoy seeing this film?

Using the interrogative pronouns below, write five sentences that belong under each title.

The Big Game
1. Who Answers will vary.
2. Whom
3. Whose
4. What
5. Which

An Effective Punishment
1. Who Answers will vary.
2. Whom
3. Whose
4. What
5. Which

Page 27

Pearls

Relative pronouns are used to introduce groups of words that modify nouns. **Interrogative pronouns** introduce a question.
relative pronouns: who, whose, which, that
People who read a lot are often very intelligent.
interrogative pronouns: who, whom, whose, what, which
Whose book is this?

Circle the relative pronouns in the paragraph.

The book (that) I read for my report really made me think. *The Pearl*, (which) was written by John Steinbeck, is a parable about survival and overcoming oppression. I am one (who) has faced little prejudice in my life, yet there are many other people (who) struggle their entire lives to break free of injustice. These men and women, (whose) lives exemplify the test of perseverance, inspire me. I appreciate the story (that) Steinbeck told, (which) demonstrates very well the power of oppression and the importance of perseverance.

Underline all the relative and interrogative pronouns in the sentences below. Write an I if it is interrogative or an R if it is relative.

I 1. Whose pearl necklace is this?
R 2. She wore pearls that were creamy white.
R 3. My mom, who is a pearl lover, owns many beautiful pieces of pearl jewelry.
R 4. A perfect pearl, which is formed in an oyster, can be extremely valuable.
I 5. Which color pearl do you prefer?
I 6. Hey, to whom does this pearl necklace belong?
R 7. I prefer black pearls, which are beautiful and unusual.
R 8. Pearls that are cultivated naturally are rare.
I 9. Who wants to dive for pearls?
I 10. What makes a pearl valuable?

Page 28

G-nip, G-nop

Reflexive pronouns are formed by adding ***self*** or ***selves*** to certain forms of personal pronouns. They reflect the action of the verb back to the subject. **Intensive pronouns** are formed in the same way, but they give intensity back to the noun or pronoun just named.
reflexive: *I taught **myself** to play table tennis.*
intensive: *The table **itself** comes from the sporting shop down the street.*

Underline the reflexive and intensive pronouns in the sentences below. Write an R if it is a reflexive pronoun; write an I if it is intensive.

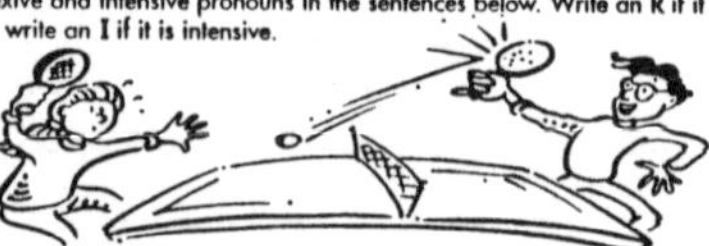

R 1. We all taught ourselves to play table tennis.
I 2. The table itself stands in our basement.
I 3. Dad himself carried it downstairs on Andrew's eleventh birthday.
I 4. I myself couldn't wait to grab a paddle and start playing.
R 5. The boys immediately placed themselves around the game table.
R 6. Christina proclaimed herself to be a pro.
R 7. You are probably asking yourself who actually played the first game.
I 8. It was Mom herself who made the first challenge.
I 9. My father himself quickly accepted it, and they began to play.
R 10. They played themselves into an intensely competitive sweat.
R 11. We took turns teaching ourselves to volley the ball back and forth.
I 12. I myself like the game so much that I can play for hours each day.

Write two sentences that include reflexive pronouns and two sentences that include intensive pronouns.

(reflexive) 1. Answers will vary.
(reflexive) 2. ______
(intensive) 1. ______
(intensive) 2. ______

Page 29

The Case of the Missing Cow

The use of **who** and **whom** is determined by the pronoun's function in the clause. Generally, **who** is used as the subject of a sentence or a clause. **Whom** is used as the object (direct, indirect, or object of the preposition).
*With **whom** did you see the cow last night?*
***Who** is a suspect?*

Read the sentences below and circle the correct pronoun.

1. Farmer Frank is the one (who, whom) owns the cow. — who
2. Steve Grant is the officer in (who, whom) Farmer Frank has placed his trust to find her. — whom
3. Do you know (who, whom) has taken Farmer Frank's cow, Bessie? — who
4. Farmer Frank's wife, (who, whom) gave the cow as a gift, has been crying since Bessie's disappearance. — who
5. (Who, Whom) would want a huge plastic cow anyway? — Who
6. The police at the station to (who, whom) she spoke have tried to calm her down. — whom
7. There is a rumor that someone (who, whom) is planning a harmless prank has taken the plastic bovine. — who
8. To (who, whom) was this information given? — whom
9. Mrs. McGrady is the one (who, whom) heard that the cow might show up on the high school roof. — who
10. She did not know (who, whom) might be instigating such a stunt. — who
11. The students (who, whom) attend Dairyville High are being questioned. — who
12. No one seems to know anything about those (who, whom) are involved. — who
13. Farmer Frank released a statement saying that he was not angry with the pranksters (who, whom) have borrowed his cow, but he is asking that they return her unharmed. — who
14. Officer Grant is the one with (who, whom) you should speak if you have any information about Bessie the missing cow. — whom

Using **who** and **whom**, write a paragraph explaining the solution to the case of the missing cow.

Answers will vary.

Page 30

Little Boy Blue

A **verb** is a word that expresses action or a state of being.
action: *go, jump, breathe, love, break*
state of being: *is, are, look, seem*
action: *Little Boy Blue **deserted** his toys.*
state of being: *The little boy **is** blue.*

Underline the verbs in this poem written by Eugene Field. Mark them A (action) or S (state of being).

Little Boy Blue

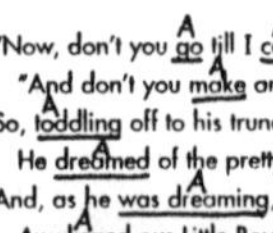

The little toy dog is (S) covered with dust,
But sturdy and staunch he stands (A);
And the little toy soldier is (S) red with rust,
And his musket molds (A) in his hands.
Time was (S) when the little toy dog was (S) new,
And the soldier was (S) passing fair;
And that was (S) the time when our Little Boy Blue
Kissed (A) them and put (A) them there.

"Now, don't you go (A) till I come (A)," he said (A),
"And don't you make (A) any noise!"
So, toddling (A) off to his trundle bed,
He dreamed (A) of the pretty toys;
And, as he was dreaming (A), an angel song
Awakened (A) our Little Boy Blue—
Oh! the years are (S) many, the years are (S) long,
But the little toy friends are (S) true!

Aye, faithful to Little Boy Blue they stand (A),
Each in the same old place—
Awaiting (A) the touch of a little hand,
The smile of a little face;
And they wonder (A), as waiting (A) the long years through
In the dust of that little chair,
What has become (S) of our Little Boy Blue,
Since he kissed (A) them and put (A) them there.

—Eugene Field (1850–1895)

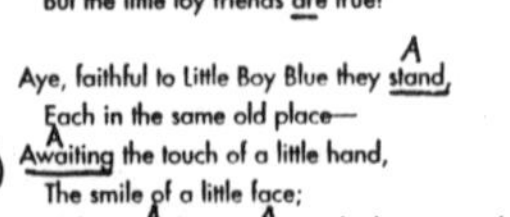

Page 31

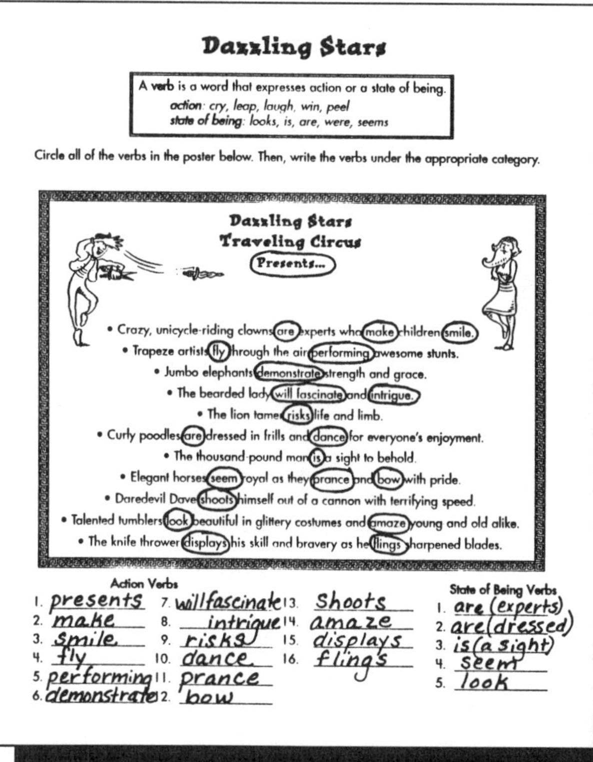

Dazzling Stars

A **verb** is a word that expresses action or a state of being.
action: cry, leap, laugh, win, peel
state of being: looks, is, are, were, seems

Circle all of the verbs in the poster below. Then, write the verbs under the appropriate category.

Dazzling Stars
Traveling Circus
Presents...

- Crazy, unicycle-riding clowns are experts who make children smile.
- Trapeze artists fly through the air performing awesome stunts.
- Jumbo elephants demonstrate strength and grace.
- The bearded lady will fascinate and intrigue.
- The lion tamer risks life and limb.
- Curly poodles are dressed in frills and dance for everyone's enjoyment.
- The thousand-pound man is a sight to behold.
- Elegant horses seem royal as they prance and bow with pride.
- Daredevil Dave shoots himself out of a cannon with terrifying speed.
- Talented tumblers look beautiful in glittery costumes and amaze young and old alike.
- The knife thrower displays his skill and bravery as he flings sharpened blades.

Action Verbs

1. presents
2. make
3. smile
4. fly
5. performing
6. demonstrate
7. will fascinate
8. intrigue
9. risks
10. dance
11. prance
12. bow
13. shoots
14. amaze
15. displays
16. flings

State of Being Verbs

1. are (experts)
2. are (dressed)
3. is (a sight)
4. seem
5. look

Page 32

Volcanoes

A **verb** must agree with its **subject** in number. A singular subject requires a singular verb, and a plural subject requires a plural verb. **Note:** The number of a subject is not changed by a phrase or a clause that might follow it.

singular: The volcano erupts. *The volcano, which has looked threatening for hours, erupts.*
plural: The volcanoes erupt. *The volcanoes that line the mountaintop erupt.*

In the following sentences, circle the correct verb.

1. Volcanic eruptions (occur, occurs) when magma (rise, rises) through the earth's crust and emerges onto the surface.
2. Magma that (erupt, erupts) onto the earth's surface (is, are) called lava.
3. Just about all types of lava (contain, contains) silicon and oxygen.
4. When lava flows over the earth, the land that lies in its path (is destroyed, are destroyed).
5. Most Hawaiian eruptions (is, are) gentle.
6. Some others (blast, blasts) huge amounts of volcanic ash high into the air.
7. After a powerful blast, volcanic ash (settle, settles) everywhere.
8. Volcanic islands (emerge, emerges) from the ocean when ash and lava (build, builds) up over years.
9. Legend (say, says) that when Pele the volcano goddess becomes angry, she causes volcanoes to erupt.

Write subjects that agree with the following verbs. Answers will vary.

________ swing	________ stay	________ have
________ eats	________ tell	________ is
________ shows	________ are	________ cares

Write verbs that agree with the following subjects.

restaurants ________	pirates ________	car ________
ladders ________	children ________	videos ________
frog ________	snow ________	facts ________

Page 33

Chocolate

The **tense** of a verb indicates the time in which an action takes place.
Present tense indicates action or being that is happening now.
*I **eat** chocolate kisses.*
Past tense indicates action or being that was completed in the past.
*I **ate** chocolate kisses.*
Future tense indicates action or being that will take place in the future. The auxiliary verb *will* is usually used with the principal verb to form the future tense.
*I **will eat** chocolate kisses.*

Underline the verb in each sentence. Identify the tense of each verb by marking **P** (present tense), **PA** (past tense), or **F** (future tense).

F 1. I will always love every kind of chocolate.
P 2. Delicious chocolate comes from bumpy green pods on tropical trees in Central and South America.
PA 3. Chocolate beans were as valuable to the Aztecs as money.
PA 4. The trees were called *kakahuatl* (ca-ca-hoo-AH-tul) by the Aztec.
P 5. Today the kakahuatl tree is called the cacao (cah-cow) tree.
PA 6. Only rich Aztecs drank chocolatl (show-co-lah-tul).
P 7. Cacao trees are grown in tropical countries around the world.
P 8. Cacao trees have long, shiny, bright green leaves with bunches of little flowers on their football-shaped pods.
P 9. A cacoa pod contains 20–40 semi-purple beans.
P 10. The cacao beans are bitter.
F 11. Then they will be dried in the sun.
F 12. These special beans will eventually become chocolate liquor.

Page 34

Origami Bird

An **infinitive** is a present tense verb preceded by the word *to* (to + verb). An infinitive can act as a noun, an adjective, or an adverb.
*George sat on the front step **to finish** his paper bird.*

Underline all of the infinitives in the directions for creating an origami bird.

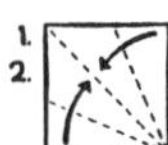

1. It is easy to create an origami bird, but you must be careful to follow the directions exactly.
2. To begin, you must cut out a perfect square (6" or about 15 cm is good) of paper. Then fold the outer edges to the middle on the dotted lines as shown.

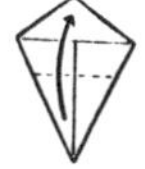

3. Now your paper should resemble a kite. Fold the "kite" in half in order to touch the top corner to the bottom corner.
4. Fold the tip down to form a beak.
5. To continue, fold your paper back, as shown, on the dotted lines.
6. Your bird will begin to appear when you pull the beak out and the neck begins to move up at the same time.
7. Press the paper firmly at the stars to make the neck stay in place.

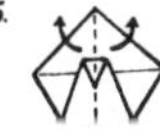

8. It is important to fold the bottom points up on each side to add feet to your creation.
9. Try again by using different colors and sizes of paper to design dozens of origami birds.

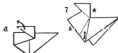

Page 35

Cooking Up a Storm

An **infinitive** is a present tense verb usually preceded by *to*. It is often used as a noun serving as a subject or a predicate noun. An infinitive phrase includes modifiers, a complement, or a subject, which act together as a single part of speech.

subject: ***To make dinner*** *for Grandma was Lesley's reason for taking a cooking class.*
predicate noun: *Lesley's hope is* ***to make a seven-course meal.***

Underline the infinitives or infinitive phrases in each of the following sentences.

1. To cook is my grandma's favorite hobby.
2. She likes to shop for interesting ingredients.
3. I was hoping to visit her after school.
4. One of my goals is to learn to make meatballs like Grandma's.
5. To make spaghetti is Grandma Elsie's specialty.
6. Her favorite kitchen experience is to create chocolate-covered cream puffs.
7. According to my grandma, the key to becoming a good cook is to practice.
8. To watch my grandma in the kitchen is very entertaining.
9. She always seems to make a big mess before her masterpieces are done.
10. To clean up the kitchen is not fun unless you are cleaning with Grandma.
11. Her quick clean-up method is to put everything in the dishwasher so that we can sit down and eat something delicious.
12. I like to cook and eat with Grandma Elsie.

In each of the following sentences, underline the infinitive phrase used as a noun and indicate if it is a subject (S) or a predicate noun (PN).

S 1. To give a great party was Candy's plan.
S 2. To write the guest list was her first priority.
PN 3. Her next step was to plan the menu and decorations.
PN 4. Her idea was to celebrate with a Hawaiian theme.
S 5. To offer her guests grass skirts and leis seemed like a good idea.
S 6. To hula dance would also be a fun activity.
S 7. To view her work hours later gave her pleasure.
PN 8. All that was left was to enjoy the party.

Page 36

Riddle Me This

The mood of the verb indicates the attitude or viewpoint behind the verb's expression. The **imperative mood** indicates a command or a request. The subject is always *you*, though this is not always expressed.

Please, wake me up at 7:00.
Make up your mind.

Write Y in the space if the sentence uses the imperative mood. Write N if it does not.

Y 1. Mow the lawn.
Y 2. Quiet down, please.
N 3. She dances gracefully.
N 4. The pizza is hot.
Y 5. Go outside to play.
N 6. The flowers smell nice.
Y 7. Wait for me!
N 8. Mustard tastes gross.
Y 9. Just behave yourself.
Y 10. Please pass the salt.
N 11. He's coming home now.
Y 12. Take the garbage out.

For each riddle below, write your own answer using the imperative mood. Remember to write a command or a request.

1. What did the tired light say?
   Answers will vary.
2. What did the whistling teapot say?
3. What did the chicken's mother say before he crossed the road?
4. What did the flowers say to the lady shopping at the greenhouse?
5. What did Santa say to the elves?
6. What kind of assignment is given to the people who go to the mall?

Page 37

"Eggs"tremely Active

A verb is in the **active voice** when the subject of the sentence is performing the action.

The bird ***laid*** *an egg.*
A large speckled egg ***hatched.***

In the following paragraph, underline each simple subject and circle each active voice verb.

Hen's eggs take just twenty-one days to hatch. The hen must sit on her eggs to keep them warm until the chicks are born. Inside the egg, yolk and white provide nourishment for the bird. A red spot on the yolk will turn into a chick after three weeks. Tiny organs such as a beak and a stomach form. The wings and feet develop too. Sticky feathers cover the chick, and the chick's egg tooth forms. Tiny holes in the egg's shell allow air to pass in and out. The chick's head lies near an air pocket at one end of the egg. The chick pushes its beak into the pocket to get its first breath of air. The chick uses its sharp egg tooth to break out of its shell. Finally, the baby bird dries and fluffs its yellow feathers and begins its search for food.

Read the numbered sentences below and underline the active voice verbs.

1. As an adult, a chicken's weight ranges from about 1.1 pounds (.5 kg) to more than 11 pounds (5 kg).
2. Feathers, which cover most of the body, will keep the chicken warm in cold weather.
3. A chicken's feathers also come in a range of colors and patterns.
4. Unlike some other birds, chickens develop fleshy structures called the comb and wattle.
5. These structures keep the chicken cool and help in recognition.
6. The shape and size of the comb vary from breed to breed.

Page 38

Around the World with Sweets

When the subject is receiving the action, a **passive voice** verb is being used.

The sweet treats ***were enjoyed*** *by everyone.*

In the following sentences, underline the passive voice verbs. Then, rewrite each sentence using the active voice.

1. Tamarind (tam-uh-rund) is a brown, sticky treat from the tamarind pod, which is eaten by children in India.
   The children of India eat tamarind, a brown, sticky treat from the tamarind pod.
2. Tamarillos (tam-uh-RILL-oze) are tangy, red or yellow, football-shaped fruits, which are enjoyed by New Zealanders.
   New Zealanders enjoy tamarillos, tangy, red or yellow, football-shaped fruits.
3. In the Caribbean, a sweet treat called sugar cane is enjoyed by many.
   Many in the Caribbean enjoy a sweet treat called sugar cane.
4. In South America, green, heart-shaped cherimoyas (chair-ee-MOY-yuz) are favored by the children of Chile.
   In South America, the children of Chile favor green, heart-shaped cherimoyas.
5. A sweet and crunchy, brown root, called jicama (hee-kuh-mah), is served by the people of Mexico.
   The people of Mexico serve jicama, a sweet and crunchy, brown root.
6. The breadfruit, a tropical fruit that tastes like baked bread, has been made a favorite by natives of the Pacific Islands.
   Natives of the Pacific Islands have made breadfruit, a tropical fruit that tastes like baked bread, a favorite.
7. Pomegranates, round fruits with red, leathery rinds, have been cultivated throughout the Mediterranean world for a very long time.
   The Mediterranean world has cultivated pomegranates, round fruits with red, leathery rinds, for a very long time.

Page 39

The Scavenger Hunt

A verb is in the **active voice** when the subject performs the action. A verb is in the **passive voice** when the subject receives the action. (Passive voice should be used sparingly. Active voice expresses action in a natural, more direct way.)

active voice: We played the scavenger hunt game at school.
passive voice: The scavenger hunt game was played by us at school.

Identify the verbs in the following sentences by labeling them A (active) or P (passive). If the verb is in passive voice, rewrite the sentence, changing the verb to active voice.

P 1. The scavenger hunt game was played by the entire class.
The entire class played the scavenger hunt game.

P 2. The class was divided into two teams by Mr. Mack, our homeroom teacher.
Mr. Mack, our home room teacher, divided the class into two teams.

A 3. We called our team "The Scavengers."

A 4. The other team gave themselves the name "The Search Party."

P 5. All of the clues were carefully hidden by our teacher.
Our teacher carefully hid all of the clues.

P 6. At the beginning of the game, each team was given the first clue by Mr. Mack.
At the beginning of the game, Mr. Mack gave each team the first clue.

A 7. We found it hidden by the drinking fountain next to the principal's office.

P 8. After a long and challenging hunt for clues, the game was finally won by "The Search Party."
After a long and challenging hunt for clues, "The Search Party" finally won the game.

Page 40

No-Bake Cookies

A **regular verb** is one which forms its past tense and past participle by adding *d* or *ed* to the present tense verb form. An **irregular verb** is any verb which does not form its past and past participle by adding *d* or *ed* to its present tense.

	present	past	past participle
regular	bake	baked	(have, has, had) baked
irregular	eat	ate	(have, has, had) eaten

In the recipe below, circle the verbs. Then, write each verb and its forms in the proper column below.

Combine 2 cups (480 ml) sugar, 1/2 cup (120 ml) milk, 1/2 cup (120 ml) butter, 1/2 cup (120 ml) cocoa in a 2-quart (1.9 l) saucepan. Place the pan on the burner at medium heat. Stir constantly. Bring to a boil; boil for one minute. Remove from heat and add 1/2 cup (120 ml) smooth peanut butter, 2 teaspoons (10 ml) vanilla, and 3 cups (720 ml) dry oatmeal. Mix ingredients together well. Tear a large piece of wax paper from the roll and lay it on the counter top away from the heat. On the wax paper, drop spoonfuls of the mixture. Chill the cookies in the refrigerator for quick results.

Regular Verbs

	present	past	past participle
1.	Combine	combined	combined
2.	place	placed	placed
3.	stir	stirred	stirred
4.	boil	boiled	boiled
5.	remove	removed	removed
6.	add	added	added
7.	mix	mixed	mixed
8.	drop	dropped	dropped
9.	chill	chilled	chilled

Irregular Verbs

	present	past	past participle
1.	bring	brought	brought
2.	tear	tore	torn
3.	lay	laid	laid
4.	let	let	let

Page 41

So Weird!

An **irregular verb** is any verb that does not follow the *d* or *ed* pattern for forming its past and past participle.

	present	past	past participle
regular verb	jump	jumped	(have, has, had) jumped
irregular verb	go	went	(have, has, had) gone

For each of the irregular verbs below, write the missing forms. You may need to refer to your grammar text for help with some of the answers.

Present	Past	Past Participle (have, has, or had)
think	thought	thought
spend	spent	spent
drive	drove	driven
begin	began	begun
eat	ate	eaten
fall	fell	fallen
hide	hid	hidden
write	wrote	written
speak	spoke	spoken
hear	heard	heard
tear	tore	torn
take	took	taken
weave	wove	woven
steal	stole	stolen
choose	chose	chosen

Write a sentence for each tense of the irregular verb *fly*.

(present) 1. Answers will vary.

(past) 2.

(past participle) 3.

Page 42

Anna Advice

A **verb phrase** is a group of words that does the work of a single verb. The phrase includes one principal verb and one or more helping verbs (usually forms of *to be*).

Anna Advice ***has been giving*** *good advice for years.*

In the letter below, underline all of the verb phrases and circle the helping verbs.

Dear Anna Advice,

I have been trying to make a difficult decision, and I am hoping you can help me out. All of my friends are planning to go skiing next weekend, and they want me to go along too. The problem is that I have been skiing before and have hated it. I was totally terrified by the ski lift (I guess I was afraid of heights or something), and I was freaked out when I literally flew down the hill completely out of control. I had vowed I would never go skiing again, but now I am feeling like a baby and am wondering what I should do. Please help.

Sincerely,
Afraid to Swoosh in Pennsylvania

Dear Afraid to Swoosh,

I have been considering your dilemma carefully and have finally concluded that you should be honest with your friends. I would bet that they will understand how you are feeling. Certainly you could join them on the skiing trip but skip the skiing. Who knows, maybe another one of your friends is having the same concern! I am sure you will have a great time!

Sincerely,
Anna Advice

Page 43

Giant Pandas

A **linking verb** does not show action. It connects the subject of the sentence to a word or words in the predicate. Forms of the word *to be* are the most common linking verbs, but other words can serve to join the ideas in a sentence as well. Any verb that can be substituted by a form of *to be* is a linking verb.

Pandas **are** *enormous animals.*

Ming Ling **felt** soft.

In each of the following sentences, underline the linking verb and circle the words in the subject and the predicate that are joined (or connected) by it.

1. Giant pandas seem friendly and harmless.
2. They are very beautiful and look like cuddly teddy bears.
3. The giant panda is a native of the dense bamboo forests of China.
4. The Chinese people are extremely proud of pandas and have made them a symbol of their country.
5. Bamboo is the panda's primary food; it makes up almost 99 percent of the bear's diet.
6. Thousands of years ago, bamboo forests were bountiful in eastern China, and giant pandas dwelled there.
7. The biggest panda ever weighed was almost 400 pounds (182 kg), but the average panda weighs over 200 pounds (91 kg).
8. Panda cubs can be very small weighing only about 5 ounces (140 g).
9. The bones of a panda are large, thick, and very heavy.
10. Pandas seem very happy in their lush, green habitat.
11. Pandas in the zoo are a pleasure to watch.
12. Unfortunately, giant pandas are among the most endangered animals on the earth today.

Page 44

Greeny

A **linking verb** does not show action. It connects the subject of the sentence to a word or words in the predicate. Commonly used linking verbs are forms of *to be*. Other linking verbs include *grow, become, appear, taste,* and *remain*. If you can substitute a form of *to be* for a verb, it is probably a linking verb.

The plant ***was*** *tall.*
The plant ***appeared*** *tall.*

Underline the linking verb in each sentence and circle the word or words that it links.

Greeny

Greeny the bean plant, appeared as a bud.
He remained rather small and was labeled a dud.
The warm rains then fell 'till the sun appeared bright.
Greeny the bean plant said, I'll be all right.
Watch me become big, straight, and tall.
I'm no longer look little but biggest of all."
Soon he was proud to lie on a plate.
And, the diners agreed, He tastes perfectly great!

Write sentences about vegetables using the following linking verbs.

1. (look) Answers will vary.
2. (become) ________
3. (appear) ________
4. (taste) ________
5. (remain) ________

Page 45

Mighty Minerals

A **subject complement** is a word that comes after a linking verb and refers back to the subject. Subject complements can be nouns, pronouns, or adjectives. A noun used as a subject complement is called a **predicate noun.** When a pronoun is used, it is called a **predicate pronoun**. An adjective used as a subject complement is called a **predicate adjective.**

predicate noun: *The ruby is a* ***gem.***
predicate pronoun: *The ruby is* ***it.***
predicate adjective: *The ruby is* ***red.***

In the following sentences, circle all of the subject complements. Then, draw an arrow from the subject complement to the subject and underline the linking verb. On the line, write PN for predicate noun, PPN for predicate pronoun, and PA for predicate adjective.

PN 1. A person who studies minerals is a mineralogist.
PA 2. Minerals are useful.
PN 3. Minerals that make metals are ore minerals.
PA 4. All minerals are uniquely beautiful.
PA 5. Emeralds are green.
PN 6. One very strong mineral is the diamond.
PPN 7. If you're looking for a very hard mineral, the diamond is it.
PA 8. No mineral is harder.
PA 9. Graphite, however, is very soft.
PPN 10. The black substance in a pencil that leaves a mark on paper is it.
PN 11. One property of minerals is specific gravity.
PA 12. Having a very high specific gravity, gold ore is extremely heavy.
PA 13. The hobby of mineral collecting is popular.
PN 14. Occasionally, obtaining certain minerals is a challenge.
PN 15. Minerals are the most common solid materials on earth.

Page 46

For the Love of Insects

A **transitive verb** is an action verb that is followed by a direct object. The verb "transmits" the action from the subject to the object. The direct object can be found by asking *what* or *whom* after the verb.

Insects ***fill*** *our world.* (S, DO)
Many insects ***help*** *man, but some insects* ***destroy*** *gardens.* (S, DO, S, DO)

In each of the sentences in the paragraph, underline the transitive verbs and label the direct objects with a DO.

Most insects eat plants (DO). Some feed on roots or decaying plant life. The majority of insects favor stems (DO) and leaves (DO), but some species devour other insects (DO). Dragonflies catch mosquitos (DO), midges, and small moths. Some giant waterbugs catch fish (DO) twice their own size. A praying mantis will "pray" motionless for hours before snaring an insect (DO). The helpful ladybug eliminates pesky aphids (DO) each time it dines.

People dislike insects (DO) for various reasons, however. Destructive insects annihilate crops (DO), and others carry terrible diseases (DO). Often people spray poisonous insecticides (DO) to control the troublemakers. Unfortunately, insecticides harm helpful insects (DO) as well. Today, scientists seek better solutions (DO) to our insect problems while they rely on the many useful insects to help them out.

In the numbered sentences below, underline the direct object and draw a line from the transitive verb to the direct object.

1. Scientists have discovered about one million species of insects.
2. Insects pollinate many of our crops and provide us with honey and other products.
3. Like humans, insects build bridges, apartment buildings, and homes.
4. They also raise crops and keep "livestock."
5. Scientists estimate the average number of insects per square mile of land equals the number of people on earth!
6. The insect world encompasses some of the most attractive and fascinating animals on earth.

Page 47

Morning Munchies

An **intransitive verb** does not need a direct object to complete its meaning. It does not direct action toward an object or a person. An intransitive verb is frequently followed by a prepositional phrase.

The cereal ***was eaten*** *in the morning.*

In the sentences on the cereal box below, underline the intransitive verbs and circle the subjects. Write the intransitive verbs you find on the lines to the right.

Morning Munchies

Finally, a cereal for the morning munchies has arrived! When toast or frozen waffles won't cut it, *Morning Munchies* will. Inside each box, the flavor waits. The crunch of sweetened nuts, along with the chew of dried fruits satisfies everytime. Even covered with milk, this breakfast sensation crunches. Other breakfast cereals fear for their future, but *Morning Munchies* worries about nothing. Although the popularity of other cereals may fade away, *Morning Munchies* will remain. Great-tasting and super-crunchy *Morning Munchies* works for everyone. So, when your hunger strikes, fill up on *Morning Munchies*.

has arrived
waits
satisfies
crunches
fear
worries
fade
will remain
works
strikes

Page 48

Gone Fishin'

A **transitive verb** is an action verb that is followed by a direct object. The verb "transmits" the action from the subject to the object. An **intransitive verb** does not need an object to complete its meaning. It is frequently followed by a prepositional phrase.

transitive: *We caught a fish.*
intransitive: *I fish with my dad.*

In the spaces below, write T if the sentence contains a transitive verb; write IT if it contains an intransitive verb. Then, underline the subject and the object (if one is present).

IT 1. Live bait wiggles in the covered container.
T 2. I am wearing my new fishing hat.
T 3. Dad stocked the tackle box with all of our gear.
T 4. We packed a sack lunch of sandwiches and apples.
T 5. I prefer fishing in the boat.
IT 6. Dad usually fishes from the pier.
T 7. We catch perch and catfish.
IT 8. Our catch is placed in a wire mesh basket.
IT 9. The sun shines brightly in the sky.
T 10. I will probably get a sunburn today.
T 11. I really don't mind baiting my own hook.
IT 12. Dad smiles at me.
T 13. Before we head home, I want to catch a super-big fish.
T 14. Dad throws back a big, ugly dogfish.
IT 15. We will definitely brag about our fishing conquests.
T 16. My dad likes fishing with a girl like me.

Page 49

Duke's Dilemma

Lie means to recline, to rest, or to remain in a reclining position. The principal parts of *lie* are *lie, lay, (have, has, had) lain.* **Lay** means to put something down or to place something somewhere. Its principal parts are *lay, laid, (have, has, had) laid.* This verb always has an object.

lie: *His pets* ***lie*** *on the carpet waiting for him to arrive.*
lay: *When he arrives, he* ***lays*** *a treat for each of them on the floor.*

Circle the correct verb in each of the following sentences.

1. Fiffi often (lays, **lies**) on the cushion in the bay window, letting the sun's rays warm her.
2. Her toy mouse is (**laying**, lying) nearby.
3. She meows happily when Mrs. McGregor (**lays**, lies) a bowl of milk in the corner.
4. She (**lays**, lies) a kitty snack near the bowl, too.
5. While the cat enjoys the treat, Duke, the dog, (lays, **lies**) lazily on his rug in front of the fireplace.
6. Fiffi has never (laid, **lain**) in Duke's chosen spot.
7. Once, when Mrs. McGregor had (lain, **laid**) Duke's favorite rug in a different spot, the dog whimpered and growled for hours.
8. Fiffi was so nervous, she could not (lay, **lie**) comfortably anywhere.
9. Fiffi (**lay**, laid) in the windowsill meowing unhappily.
10. As soon as Mr. McGregor came home, he removed his shoes and (lay, **laid**) his hat on the table.
11. He noticed immediately that Duke was not (laying, **lying**) in his usual spot.
12. Mr. McGregor promptly (lay, **laid**) Duke's rug in its usual location.
13. A relieved Duke instantly (**lay**, laid) down and closed his eyes.
14. As for Fiffi, she was once again able to (lay, **lie**) peacefully on the window seat in the sunshine.
15. Mr. McGregor (laid, **lay**) in his recliner and watched the football game.

Page 50

Set the Table, Sit for Tea

The verb **sit** means to assume a sitting position or to occupy a seat. The principal parts of *sit* are *sit, sat, (have, has, had) sat.* The verb **set** means to put something in position or to make something rigid. The principal parts of *set* are *set, set, (have, has, had) set.*

sit: *She likes to* ***sit*** *in the chair by the window.*
set: *She* ***set*** *her tea on the ledge by the window.*

Circle the correct verb in each of the following sentences.

1. Claire and I (sat, **set**) aside some time to spend with Mrs. Fargate, the widow who lives next door.
2. We had (sat, **set**) out our best clothes for the occasion.
3. When we arrived, Mrs. Fargate asked us to come in and (set, **sit**) down.
4. Several ceramic pots filled with coral-colored geraniums were (sat, **set**) on the window ledge to create a happy atmosphere.
5. I (**sat**, set) in an overstuffed chair with green-and-white-checked cushions and looked around.
6. Clarie chose to (set, **sit**) upon a fluffy couch.
7. Mrs. Fargate's miniature poodle, Teacup, (**sat**, set) politely on the rocking chair, showing off the pink ribbon attached to the curly hair on her forehead.
8. We (**sat**, set) there together talking about trivial things.
9. Mrs. Fargate (sat, **set**) out the dishes.
10. She served us frosted lemon bars, which she (sat, **set**) on lovely linen napkins.
11. Our hostess (sat, **set**) a fine white porcelain teapot, decorated with tiny painted roses, on the coffee table.
12. Then she poured the tea into the delicate little cups that had been (sat, **set**) out for our visit.
13. Mrs. Fargate moved elegantly, (**setting**, sitting) her cup gently in the saucer.
14. We had a wonderful time (**sitting**, setting) in Mrs. Fargate's sunny parlor.

Page 51

Accepting Effective Exceptions

Don't confuse the meaning of these troublesome verbs.
accept: (v) to take what is offered
except: (prep) to leave out; other than
affect: (v) to influence; change
effect: (n) result; consequence

*We will **accept** the invitation.* *The weather may **affect** our plans.*
*Everyone **except** Joe is going.* *Hopefully, the **effect** will be good.*

Circle the correct verb to complete each of the following sentences.

On the Beat

1. Police officers (accept, except) the responsibility of enforcing the law of the land.
2. Their commitment to the job can drastically (affect, effect) the community.
3. A policeman is a friend to everyone (accept, except) the lawbreaker.
4. Going to prison is one possible (affect, effect) of committing a crime.

Green Grass of Home

1. Yes, I am willing to (accept, except) payment for a job well done.
2. I always charge at least $10.00 when I mow a lawn, (accept, except) when I mow Mrs. Kennedy's for free.
3. Rain (affects, effects) how quickly the grass grows.
4. The (affect, effect) of lots of rain is a lot of lawn-mowing work for me.

A Good Example

1. I don't mind babysitting my little sister, (accept, except) when I have other plans.
2. Since she doesn't like anyone else to watch her, babysitting my sister has begun to (affect, effect) my social life.
3. My mom always tells me that I have a good (affect, effect) on my little sister.
4. I guess I can (accept, except) that.

Brain Power

1. (Accept, Except) for Saturday and Sunday, I go to school every day.
2. All of this studying is starting to (affect, effect) my brain.
3. It's difficult for me to (accept, except) the fact that I have to study before a test.
4. But when I do, the (affect, effect) is that I usually get a good grade.

Page 52

Go Down, Moses

A **direct object** is a noun, a pronoun, or a group of words acting as a noun that receives the action of the verb. It is easy to find the direct object by asking the question *what* or *whom* **after the verb.**
*In seventh grade we study **heroes**.*
*Ask: We study whom? Answer: **heroes***

Read the sentences about Harriet Tubman and circle the direct objects. Some sentences may have more than one direct object, while other sentences may have none.

1. The courageous Harriet Tubman freed many slaves by way of the underground railroad.
2. Harriet would sing an old spiritual as a signal to the slaves to leave.
3. She was called Moses because many thought she was similar to the biblical figure.
4. The slaves would escape from the plantations in the middle of the night.
5. They desperately wanted freedom.
6. The band of fugitives traveled by foot from their southern states toward Canada.
7. While the runaways walked, Harriet told them vivid stories about freedom to calm their growing fears.
8. Many brave men and women helped to hide the fugitives on their flight to freedom.
9. Fortunately, Harriet Tubman never lost any passengers on her 19 trips on the underground railroad.
10. People issued rewards totaling $40,000 for the capture of Harriet Tubman.
11. As a spy during the Civil War, she freed more than 750 slaves.
12. Harriet Tubman risked her life to lead hundreds of men, women, and children to freedom.

Page 53

Happily Ever After

An **indirect object** is a noun or pronoun that names the person *to whom* or *for whom* something is done. To find the indirect object, ask *to whom* or *for whom* after the action verb.
The Prince sang Cinderella an off-key love song.
*Question: The Prince sang an off-key love song **to whom?***
Answer: Cinderella

In each of the following sentences, underline the indirect object and circle the action verb. Write the title of the fairy tale to which each sentence is referring in the corresponding box below.

1. She was bringing her grandmother a basket of goodies.
2. A man sold the little pig a bundle of sticks for building a house.
3. She left Baby Bear an empty porridge bowl.
4. They worked hard each night to make the shoemaker some leather shoes.
5. The wicked stepmother gave her many chores to do.
6. The pea hidden beneath the pile of mattresses gave her a sore back.
7. He handed his mother the magic beans.
8. The tailors made the emperor royal new garments.
9. She gave the wicked witch a push into the hot oven.
10. The handsome prince gave Sleeping Beauty a kiss to awaken her.
11. The wicked queen, dressed as an old hag, offered the girl a poisonous apple.
12. The tricky trio told the troll a lie.

1. Little Red Ridinghood	2. The Three Little Pigs	3. Goldilocks and the Three Bears	4. The Shoemaker and the Elves	5. Cinderella	6. The Princess and the Pea
7. Jack and the Beanstalk	8. The Emperor's New Clothes	9. Hansel and Gretel	10. Sleeping Beauty	11. Snow White and the Seven Dwarfs	12. The Three Billy Goats Gruff

Page 54

Collection Craze

The noun or pronoun used as the **object of the preposition** follows the preposition or prepositional phrase. A preposition relates the noun or pronoun to another word in the sentence. To find the object of the preposition, ask *whom* or *what* **after the preposition.**
Lucinda jumped over the gate.
*Lucinda jumped over what? **the gate***
Grandma sent money to us.
*Grandma sent money to whom? **us***

Read the paragraphs below. Place parentheses around the prepositional phrases and underline the objects of the preposition. Find 23 objects of the preposition.

It seems that everyone collects something these days (For some reason) collecting has become one (of America's most popular hobbies) (Aside from ordinary stamp or coin collecting) individuals (of all ages) are collecting everything (from unique pencil erasers) (to the ever-popular stuffed animals) Baseball cards have been highly collectible (for many years) but today a person can collect any kind (of card) including basketball, football, hockey, and even post cards. Books, cars, shoes, teacups, hats—a collector's possibilities are endless.

Many people are willing to spend a great deal (of money) (on their collections) A rare baseball card could cost a collector thousands (of dollars) Doll collectors often spend hundreds (of dollars) (for a single, yet desirable, piece) (for their collection) (Without a doubt) these collectors hope that over many years their treasures will increase (in value)

(In addition to expensive collectibles) there are many that cost the collector nothing (except time and effort) Some people keep greeting cards or snippets (of wrapping paper) received (on gifts) Shells, rocks, feathers, leaves, and other items (from nature) are common collector's items. Matchbooks (from restaurants) are also freebie collectibles. Collecting one's favorite things is fun, (regardless of their true value) So, join the collecting craze. After all, everybody's doing it!

Page 55

Gunky Goop

Compound prepositions are two or more words working together like a one-word preposition.

*The skiers **in front of** the fireplace were drinking hot chocolate.*

Read the advertisement for GUNKY GOOP and underline each compound preposition.

And now, a word from our sponsors . . .

According to cool kids everywhere, *GUNKY GOOP* finishes ahead of all other hair gels. Squeeze a dab of *GUNKY GOOP* out of its funky tube and you'll be blown away by its fun, fresh scent. Create crazy styles in addition to shiny looks when you use *GUNKY GOOP*. Because of its mighty holding power, *GUNKY GOOP* will keep your hair looking fine for hours. Say goodbye to geeky hair styles and bad hair days forever! Instead of using other lame gels, try *GUNKY GOOP*.

GUNKY GOOP . . .
GEL FOR KIDS WHO KNOW COOL.

List the six compound prepositions that you found.

1. according to
2. ahead of
3. out of
4. in addition to
5. because of
6. instead of

Page 56

The World of Greek Mythology

A **prepositional phrase** is a group of words that shows how two words or ideas are related to each other. It can function as an adjective or an adverb, depending on the word it modifies. Like a one-word adjective, an **adjective prepositional phrase** modifies only a noun or a pronoun.

*One ancient myth **about the rainbow goddess named Iris** captivated my attention.*

In the following sentences, underline the adjective prepositional phrases and draw an arrow to the word being modified. Make sure the prepositional phrase modifies a noun.

1. Ancient Greek stories about gods and goddesses are called myths.
2. Myths from the Greek world were created to explain the mysteries of nature.
3. Poseidon, god of the sea, was also god of earthquakes and horses.
4. The world of mythology is filled with gods, goddesses, and mortals with many marvelous powers.
5. The *Iliad* and the *Odyssey*, by Homer, contain most of the main mythological characters and themes.
6. Eros, from ancient mythology, assisted many in their quest for love.
7. Mount Olympus was the home of the major Greek gods and goddesses.
8. Zeus was a powerful Olympian in the sky and ruled over all the gods.
9. Aphrodite was known as the goddess of love and beauty.
10. Hades' home in the underworld was the land of the dead.
11. Apollo was very strong and was known as the god of music, poetry, and purity.
12. Messages for the gods were delivered by Hermes, who was swift in flight.

Page 57

The White House

Like a one-word adverb, an **adverb prepositional phrase** usually modifies a verb and may tell *where, how,* or *when* an action takes place.

*The White House is located **in Washington, D.C.*** (tells where)
*The president resides there **with his family members**.* (tells how)
*He will leave the White House **at the end of his term**.* (tells when)

In the following sentences, underline the adverb prepositional phrases and circle the words being modified. At the end of each sentence, write whether it tells **where, how,** or **when** the action takes place.

1. The West Wing was completed in 1909 and includes the new oval office. when
2. Since 1934, the Oval Office has served as the president's formal office. when
3. The president and the first lady entertain guests in the East Room. where
4. Inside the Green Room, which he used as a dining area, Thomas Jefferson placed a green cloth on the floor. where
5. The Green Room became a sitting room when it was decorated with green furnishings. how
6. The Blue Room was named by Martin Van Buren, the 8th president. how
7. The 19th-century president Rutherford B. Hayes took the oath of office in the Red Room, which is used today as a sitting room. where
8. Before state dinners, the president often entertains foreign leaders in the Yellow Oval Room. where
9. In 1941, the executive wing replaced a greenhouse complex. when
10. In the Lincoln Bedroom, the Emancipation Proclamation was signed by President Lincoln. where
11. On the second floor, the Lincoln Sitting Room adjoins the Lincoln Bedroom. where
12. A library containing many books is positioned on the ground floor. where

Page 58

Amazing Advertisements

Adjectives modify (or describe) nouns. They answer the questions *which one, what kind,* or *how many.*

*Mike's dog wears a **black leather** collar around his neck.*

Read the labels from the products below. Underline the adjectives that describe each product.

Drink the Energizer
a delicious, vitamin-filled beverage
CHEWY AND CHOCOLATEY
MONSTER CHUNK
A thick block of dark chocolate and caramel
Jazzy Jewel
Amazing Nail Polish
For healthy, glowing skin try
ZAP A ZIT
Zap those ugly zits with the new, fast-acting medicated zit cream!

Page 59

Who's Better?

A **comparative adjective** or **adverb** is used to describe a comparison between two things, people, places, or actions. A **superlative adjective** or **adverb** compares three or more things, people, places, or actions.

	positive	*comparative*	*superlative*
adjectives	*happy* *good*	*happier* *better*	*happiest* *best*
adverbs	*happily* *well*	*more/less happily* *better*	*most/least happily* *best*

Add the comparative and superlative forms of each adjective and adverb to the charts below.

Adjectives

Positive	Comparative	Superlative
new	newer	newest
durable	more/less durable	most/least durable
cheap	cheaper	cheapest
big	bigger	biggest
comfortable	m/l comfortable	m/l comfortable
beautiful	m/l beautiful	m/l beautiful
creative	m/l creative	m/l creative

Adverbs

Positive	Comparative	Superlative
proudly	more/less proudly	most/least proudly
courageously	m/l courageously	m/l courageously
quickly	m/l quickly	m/l quickly
easily	m/l easily	m/l easily
cheerfully	m/l cheerfully	m/l cheerfully
safely	m/l safely	m/l safely
slowly	m/l slowly	m/l slowly

Page 60

Touring the Zoo

This, that, these, and **those** are adjectives that modify nouns by telling *which one* or *which ones. This* and *that* are singular. *These* and *those* are plural. *This* and *these* refer to things nearby, and *that* and *those* refer to things farther away.

This zoo we are visiting is the best in the state.
That zoo across town isn't nearly as nice.
***These** animals we are seeing are cared for very well.*
***Those** animals over there are not cared for very well.*

Circle the correct form of each adjective in each of the following sentences.

1. To your immediate right you will see (this, **these**) beautiful pink flamingos.
2. Just past the trees are (these, **those**) peacocks displaying their elaborately decorated tail feathers.
3. (That, **This**) bald eagle nesting in the exhibit next to you has recently hatched an eaglet.
4. Here inside this building we see (**these**, those) handsome penguins swimming in the frigid water.
5. Over there you will see (these, **those**) marvelous white polar bears resting on the ice.
6. Right in front of you is (**this**, these) special sea lion and her cub.
7. Let's head back outside to see (these, **those**) fantastic big cats.
8. Here we see (this, **these**) sleeping lions.
9. Further down are (these, **those**) pacing tigers.
10. And way over there is (this, **that**) breathtaking snow leopard.
11. At the petting zoo, we will see (these, **those**) pigs rolling in the mud.
12. (This, **That**) flock of sheep will feel soft and woolly to the touch.
13. Inside (**this**, that) next part of the zoo, we see alligators sunning themselves.
14. Before we go, let's stop just ahead and watch (these, **those**) monkeys clown around.
15. Here we are near our last and largest zoo animal—(**this**, that) remarkable African elephant.

Page 61

Get Your Popcorn Here!

This, that, these, and *those* are **demonstrative adjectives** that point out a particular person, place, or thing. Use *this* and *these* for things close by and *that* and *those* for things distant in time or space. *This* and *that* are singular while *these* and *those* are plural.

*Look at **that** popcorn.* (singular, far) *Look at **those** candy bars.* (plural, far)
*Look at **this** popcorn.* (singular, near) *Look at **these** candy bars.* (plural, near)

Underline the demonstrative adjectives and the words they modify. Then, write each treat under the proper category below.

1. I'd like some of this cotton candy, please.
2. I'm not interested in those bags of peanuts.
3. Could you help me carry these cups of soda?
4. This pack of gummy pandas will keep my little brother happy.
5. Please grab that box of chocolates for me.
6. Look at those huge buckets of popcorn!
7. Before we go sit down, I think I'll take that box of spiced candy.
8. I think we should share these candy bars.

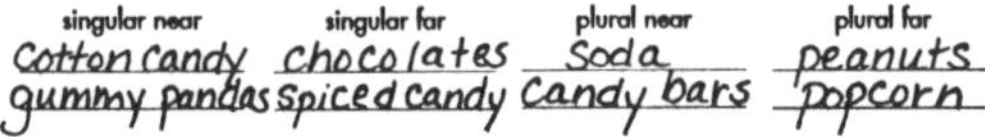

singular near	singular far	plural near	plural far
Cotton candy	chocolates	Soda	peanuts
gummy pandas	spiced candy	Candy bars	popcorn

An **indefinite adjective** is an adjective that gives an approximate number or quantity. It does not tell exactly how many or how much.
*When we go to the movies, we buy a **few** snacks to share with each other.*

In the following sentences, underline the indefinite adjectives.

1. When many friends go to the theater with me, we buy more snacks and pass them around.
2. Each person in the group buys something different to pass.
3. Some friends choose candy.
4. Of course, many people prefer to buy salty snacks to eat.
5. Soda pop is usually purchased by several movie goers.
6. After the movie, all snackers feel a little sick to their stomachs.

Page 62

Greenville Is on the Map

A **proper adjective** is an adjective formed from a proper noun. It is always capitalized and may contain more than one word.
California girls *Memorial Day parade*

Underline and capitalize all the proper adjectives from this list of locations in the small town of Greenville.

Jordan's grove	apple tree	yellow house
stop sign	soccer field	high school
Mexican restaurant	pumpkin patch	grocery store
Chinese food	Bradford's creek	new church
Patsy's pond	Joe's mail truck	flower shop
flower garden	Greenville library	fix-it shop
beauty salon	Italian ice shop	dairy farm
Siamese cat	vegetable stand	American bank
Dr. Dan's office	department store	shoe shop

Add at least one proper adjective, formed from a proper noun, for each of the items below.

1. Answers will surf shop
2. vary. bowling alley
3. __________ beach
4. __________ station
5. __________ dog

Page 63

Spelunking

A predicate adjective follows a linking verb and describes the subject.

Lanora's flashlight is (bright).

In each of the following sentences, underline the linking verb and circle the predicate adjective(s). Then draw an arrow from the predicate adjective to the subject it modifies.

1. The cave was (cold and damp).
2. Deep inside the cave it was (pitch dark) and we had to use flashlights to see where we were going.
3. Although a litter of bats hanging above us was (intimidating), none came near us.
4. The stalactites overhead were (wet).
5. They were (shiny and beautiful) like icicles.
6. The stalagmites growing out of the cave floor were (equally amazing).
7. Droplets of water falling into the nearby pools were (surprisingly noisy) in the quiet cave.
8. Several areas of the cave were (still unexplored).
9. Our tour was (very informative).
10. Underground caves are (thrilling!)

For each illustration below, write a sentence containing a subject, a linking verb, and a predicate adjective.

1. Answers will vary.
2. ______
3. ______
4. ______
5. ______

Page 64

Proverbs to Ponder

The three **articles** are *a*, *an*, and *the*. Articles are adjectives and always come before a noun. *A* and *an* are indefinite, singular articles, referring to any one of a class of nouns. The article *an* always comes before a word that begins with a vowel or a vowel sound. *A* comes before a word that begins with a consonant. *The* is definite and refers to a specific noun. It can be singular or plural.

***an** ideal place*   ***a** simple little story*   ***the** most amazing person*

In each of the proverbs below, fill in the blank with the correct article.

1. Birds of __a__ feather flock together.
2. Too many cooks spoil __the__ broth.
3. You can't teach __an__ old dog new tricks.
4. __The__ early bird catches __the__ worm.
5. One tree doesn't make __a__ forest.
6. Every cloud has __a__ silver lining.
7. __An__ apple __a__ day keeps __the__ doctor away.
8. If __the__ shoe fits, wear it.
9. __A__ picture is worth __a__ thousand words.
10. Strike while __the__ iron is hot.

Write the correct article, *a* or *an*, in front of the nouns.

__an__ actor	__a__ wreath	__an__ evening	__a__ tragedy
__a__ beauty	__a__ hospital	__an__ orchestra	__an__ honor
__an__ answer	__a__ camera	__a__ hammer	__an__ ink pen
__an__ outrage	__an__ omen	__a__ pleasure	__an__ ego

Page 65

A Really Bad Beginning

Good and *bad* are adjectives that modify nouns. *Well* and *badly* are adverbs that modify verbs.

*That was a **good** shot.* (adjective)   *He shot at that **well**.* (adverb)
*That was a **bad** shot.* (adjective)   *He shot at that **badly**.* (adverb)

Select the correct modifier in each of the following sentences.

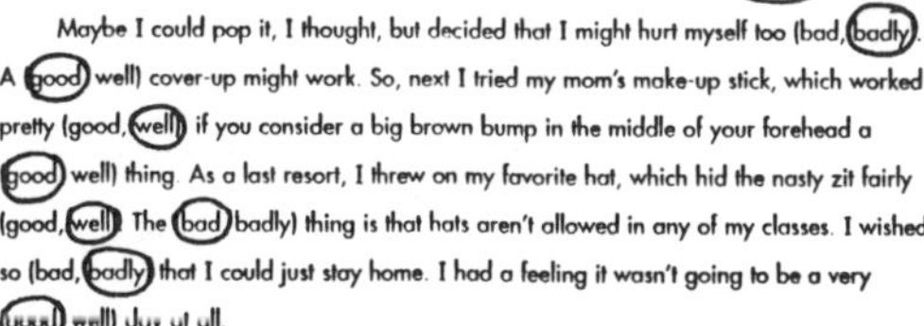

When I woke up this morning I was feeling quite (good, (well)). I went to the sink to give myself a ((good), well) teeth-brushing, but when I glanced into the mirror I saw it. There, on my forehead, was a huge red pimple, and it looked really ((bad), badly). I immediately dropped my toothbrush and reached for a comb. I tried combing my bangs straight down over the ugly thing, but that didn't work too (good, (well)). Then I tried sticking a round band-aid over it, but that didn't look very ((good), well) either. A sick sensation came over me; I felt (bad, (badly)).

Maybe I could pop it, I thought, but decided that I might hurt myself too (bad, (badly)). A ((good), well) cover-up might work. So, next I tried my mom's make-up stick, which worked pretty (good, (well)) if you consider a big brown bump in the middle of your forehead a ((good), well) thing. As a last resort, I threw on my favorite hat, which hid the nasty zit fairly (good, (well)). The ((bad), badly) thing is that hats aren't allowed in any of my classes. I wished so (bad, (badly)) that I could just stay home. I had a feeling it wasn't going to be a very ((good), well) day at all.

Page 66

The Prince Frog

An **adverb** is a word that modifies a verb, an adjective, or another adverb. Adverbs indicate **time**, **place**, or **manner**. **Adverbs of time** answer the questions *when* or *how often*. **Adverbs of place** answer the question *where*. **Adverbs of manner** answer the questions *how* or *in what manner*.

time: *Camilla slept **late**.*
place: *Camilla slept **here**.*
manner: *Camilla slept **soundly**.*

For every circled verb in the story, underline the corresponding adverb. Write the adverbs in the appropriate columns below.

Once upon a time, Camilla the frog (lived) alone in the swamp near King Ronald's castle. From her lily pad she could plainly (see) the bridge that crossed the moat surrounding the castle. Day after day, while skillfully (catching) her afternoon meal of flies, Camilla always (daydreamed) about life in a royal's world. She often (dreamt) of princesses in beautiful gowns gaily (strolling) through elegant flower gardens while young princes lazily (rested) on plush cushions by inviting little ponds. On this particular morning, Camilla decided (to venture) slowly over and finally (get) a glimpse of royal life.

Hopping across was long and difficult under the heat of the rising sun. But when she (arrived) there, Camilla instantly (saw) an unexpected and amazing sight. Under a pear-filled tree, a charming prince (lay) asleep. He was tall, dark, and handsomely (dressed) in green from head to toe. Immediately Camilla (swooned) and (drooled) as she watched the perfect creature (sleeping) nearby. Next, Camilla (leapt) to within inches of his princely face when suddenly he (stirred). She quickly (grabbed) her chance. In one move, she (jumped) up and kissed him on the lips. The dashing prince instantly (transformed) into a bumpy green frog. An elated Camilla gasped, "Here you are, my wonderful prince frog!"

Manner		Time		Place
alone	slowly	always	immediately	over
plainly	asleep	often	instantly	there
skillfully	handsomely	finally		nearby
gaily	quickly	instantly		up
lazily				

Page 67

A Close Call

Adverbs have three degrees of comparison. They are positive, comparative, and superlative. Some adverbs form the comparative degree by adding ***er*** and the superlative degree by adding ***est***. Most adverbs that end in *ly* form their comparative degrees by adding the words ***more*** or ***less*** in front of the positive degree. The superlative degree is formed by adding the words ***most*** or ***least*** in front of the positive degree.

Raquel danced less gracefully then her sisters.
I hope they will come sooner rather than later.

Write the missing adverbs in the chart.

Positive	Comparative	Superlative
fast	faster	fastest
carefully	more/less carefully	most/least carefully
soon	Sooner	Soonest
hard	harder	hardest
noisily	m/l noisily	m/l noisily
late	later	latest
easily	m/l easily	m/l easily
efficiently	m/l efficiently	m/l efficiently
loudly	m/l loudly	m/l loudly
softly	m/l softly	m/l softly
harshly	m/l harshly	m/l harshly
neatly	m/l neatly	m/l neatly
cheerfully	m/l cheerfully	m/l cheerfully
courageously	m/l courageously	m/l courageously
correctly	m/l correctly	m/l correctly

In the following sentences, circle the adverbs and indicate the degree of comparison: P (positive), C (comparative), or S (superlative).

P 1. The principal walks quickly through the halls.
C 2. David plans more intelligently than the other boys.
S 3. He dives the most gracefully behind the bleachers.
S 4. One boy leaps the least deftly and falls on his behind.
C 5. The third boy, diving more quickly than the second, makes it with only one leg hanging out.
P 6. Walking slowly across the gym floor, the principal notices the stray leg.
C 7. Hopping faster than a cricket, she pounces on the leg, pulling the boy from his spot.
S 8. David, creeping most carefully behind the bleachers, escapes to skip school another day.

Page 68

Negative Norman

A **double negative** incorrectly uses two negative words when one is sufficient. Use only one negative when you mean to say "no."

Noelle didn't want no macaroni. (incorrect)
Noelle didn't want any macaroni. (correct)

Cross out the double negatives in the following sentences. Then, rewrite each sentence so that it does not contain a double negative.

1. Negative Norman never seems to like ~~nothing~~.
Negative Norman never seems to like anything.
2. On Saturday mornings when his mom makes him pancakes, he says, "I don't want ~~none~~!"
On Saturday mornings when his mom makes him pancakes, he says, "I don't want any!"
3. When his buddies from school call, he will not talk to ~~no one~~.
When his buddies from school call, he will not talk to anyone.
4. Norman is so nasty he won't even feed his dog ~~no~~ food.
Norman is so nasty he won't even feed his dog any food.
5. All day he just sits in his bean bag chair and won't ~~never~~ go ~~nowhere~~.
All day he just sits in his bean bag chair and won't go anywhere.
6. Norman doesn't seem to have ~~no~~ smile at all.
Norman doesn't seem to have any smile at all.
7. He obviously hasn't learned ~~nothing~~ about enjoying life.
He obviously hasn't learned anything about enjoying life.
8. No one can ~~never~~ make ~~no~~ comments about his negativity ~~neither~~.
No one can ever make any comments about his negativity either.
9. Norman isn't interested in ~~no~~ know-it-all's opinions about his attitude.
Norman isn't interested in any know-it-all's opinions about his attitude.
10. Negative Norman doesn't want ~~no~~ friends, ~~no~~ fun, ~~nor no~~ advice from ~~nobody~~.
Negative Norman doesn't want any friends, any fun, or any advice from anybody.

Page 69

Ancient Pyramids

The complete subject or complete predicate of a sentence usually contains other words or phrases, called **modifiers**, that add to the meaning of the sentence.

*The ancient tombs, **which stand powerfully on the hot sands of Egypt**, are an amazing and wonderful sight.*

In the following sentences, underline the subject modifiers once and the predicate modifiers twice.

1. Ancient pyramids stand majestically in the golden desert sands of Egypt.
2. The Egyptian pyramids were erected nearly five thousand years ago.
3. Skilled craftsmen and unskilled laborers worked together to build the pyramids.
4. Brilliant architects carefully calculated and thoughtfully designed the pyramids.
5. The dangerous, difficult work of building pyramids was done slowly and carefully.
6. These incredibly large structures were built especially for the pharaohs.
7. Ancient Egyptians believed wholeheartedly in life after death.
8. The bodies of dead kings were effectively preserved and buried in the tombs.
9. Food, clothing, furniture, and jewelry that the deceased Pharaoh would need in the afterlife were buried with him.
10. Each pyramid would protect the body.
11. The embalmed body of King Khufu was once enshrined in the Great Pyramid of Giza.
12. Young King Tutankhamen was buried in royal fashion within a tomb in the Valley of the Kings.

Page 70

Locked Out

Modifiers that are not placed near the words or phrases that they modify are called **misplaced modifiers**.

***Scared to death**, the black night enveloped the lost student.* (misplaced modifier)
***Scared to death**, the lost student wandered the neighborhood in abandon.* (correct)

Underline the misplaced modifiers in the following sentences. Then, rewrite each sentence correctly.

1. After school, I have a key for getting into our locked house.
I have a key for getting into our locked house after school.
2. Under the flower pot I always know I can find an extra key.
I always know I can find an extra key under the flower pot.
3. The flower pot is missing unfortunately.
Unfortunately, the flower pot is missing.
4. In the basement, I consider breaking a window.
I consider breaking a window in the basement.
5. On the roof, I think about going down the chimney.
I think about going down the chimney on the roof.
6. Instead, I sit on the porch and wait for my mom to get home for an hour.
Instead, I sit on the porch for an hour and wait for my mom to get home.
7. We discover that the door had not even been locked when she arrives.
When she arrives, we discover that the door had not even been locked.
8. The dog barks at us as we go in through the window.
The dog barks at us through the window as we go in.

Page 71

Sand and Surf

If a modifying word, phrase, or clause does not modify a particular word, then it is called a **dangling modifier**. Every modifier must have a word that it clearly modifies.

Warmed by the sun, it felt good to be at the beach.
*(dangling modifier—"warmed by the sun" does not modify **it**)*
Warmed by the sun, we thought a day at the beach felt good.
*(correct—"warmed by the sun" does modify **we**)*

In the following sentences, underline the dangling modifier and draw an arrow to the word it is incorrectly modifying. If the modifier is used correctly, write OK in the blank.

____ 1. While running down to the water, the sand was too hot.
____ 2. Surrounded by a moat, I created a masterpiece.
OK 3. Under the umbrella, the picnic basket filled with snack foods sat.
____ 4. Reclining on the beach, sunscreen is extremely important.
OK 5. With too much sun, many sunbathers will burn.

Rewrite these sentences, correcting the dangling modifiers.

1. Riding the big waves, excited shouts emerge from the water.
Riding the big waves, they shouted excitedly from the water.
2. Lying in the sun, my suntan lotion didn't work.
Lying in the sun, I was burnt because my suntan lotion didn't work.
3. Playing barefoot, the volleyball game took place on the hot sand.
Playing barefoot, we had a volleyball game on the hot sand.
4. Tired and sandy, our beach day ended.
Tired and sandy, we ended our beach day.
5. Hanging out at the beach, the time was a lot of fun.
Hanging out at the beach, we had a lot of fun.

Page 72

Star-Crossed Lovers

A **participle** is a verb form that can function as an adjective. The **present participle** is usually formed by adding *ing* to a present tense verb. The **past participle** is usually formed by adding *ed* to the present tense. A **participial phrase** is a group of words that includes the participle and its objects, complements, or modifiers.

present participle: *Rex barks at the **passing** cars.*
past participle: *A **determined** Rex tried to chase the car.*

In each of the following sentences, identify if the participle used is a present (P) or a past (PA) participle.

P 1. Romeo's parents enquire about their moping son.
P 2. Discovering Rosaline's name on the guest list, Benvolio encourages Romeo to "crash" the Capulet party.
P 3. Wearing a mask, Romeo arrives at the party.
P 4. There he sees the smiling Juliet and longs to meet her.
P 5. The dancing couple fall hopelessly in love.
PA 6. Struck by love, Juliet is distressed to learn that Romeo belongs to the house of Montague.
P 7. The feuding Montagues and Capulets hate each other.
P 8. Appearing on the balcony, Juliet declares her passion for Romeo.
PA 9. Overheard by Romeo, her words of love inspire him.
PA 10. Soon, a determined Romeo appeals to the friar to marry the couple immediately.
P 11. Standing before the friar, the young lovers are married in secret.
P 12. Later, Romeo finds the quarreling Benvolio and Mercutio in the public square and ultimately kills Tybalt.
PA 13. Romeo is banished to Mantua while a mourning Juliet seeks help from the friar.
PA 14. Committed to being reunited with her husband, Juliet carries out a dangerous plan.
PA 15. Deceived by his sleeping lover, Romeo drinks the poison.
P 16. An awakening Juliet discovers her dying Romeo and tragically stabs herself to join him in death.

Page 73

Chores

A **gerund** is a verb form ending in *ing* that functions as a noun. Gerunds are formed by adding *ing* to the present tense verb form. A **gerund phrase** is a group of words that includes a gerund and its related words.

gerund: *Dancing is my favorite form of exercise.*
gerund phrase: ***Dancing the polka** is a good workout.*

In each of the following sentences, underline the gerund or gerund phrase and indicate how it is being used in the sentence: **S** (subject), **DO** (direct object), **OP** (object of a preposition), or **PN** (predicate noun).

S 1. Cleaning is the worst job.
DO 2. I prefer cooking.
OP 3. Sometimes I avoid my chores by complaining.
PN 4. Another strategy is procrastinating.
S 5. Vacuuming isn't so bad.
DO 6. I hate dusting.
DO 7. Occasionally, the windows need washing.
S 8. Mopping makes the floors shine.
DO 9. My room appears messy when the bed needs making.
S 10. Mowing the lawn can be relaxing work.
OP 11. I'm not fond of pulling weeds when it is scorching hot outside.
S 12. Washing dishes is a job my sister and I share.
PN 13. A disgusting chore is scrubbing the toilet.
OP 14. We never worry about polishing the silver.
S 15. Feeding the cat has been my little brother's only chore.
OP 16. Everyone in our house is responsible for folding laundry.
DO 17. Dad mainly likes fixing things.
PN 18. The best part of a chore is finishing the job.

Page 74

Medieval Times

Use a comma to separate an **introductory phrase** or **clause** from the rest of the sentence. Oftentimes these phrases will contain a preposition.

Because I am sick, I will not be able to attend the medieval festival at the park.

Underline the introductory phrase or clause in each of the following sentences. Then, add the proper punctuation to each one.

1. During the Middle Ages, the European form of government was feudalism.
2. At that time in European history, there were many fiefs, estates of feudal lords.
3. In return for his loyalty, a nobleman was provided with land by the king.
4. Under the feudal system, the owner of a fief was often a lord whose land was inhabited by people who promised to serve him.
5. When a person controlled land, he also had political, economic, judicial, and military power.
6. At the age of about seven, many young boys left home to train for knighthood.
7. As soon as a squire had mastered the necessary skills, he became a knight.
8. As a knight, a nobleman was a soldier for the king when necessary.
9. Because they had few rights, peasants were at the mercy of their lords.
10. In return for clerical services, many lords gave fiefs to the church.

Write an introductory phrase or clause for each of the following sentence endings. Add the proper punctuation.

1. Answers will vary. preparations for the feast began.
2. ____ the manor had to be cleaned.
3. ____ large amounts of elaborate foods were prepared.
4. ____ trumpets announced the arrival of the king.
5. ____ all the guests enjoyed a feast fit for a king.

Page 75

At the Carnival

An **independent clause** is a group of words with a subject and a predicate that expresses a complete thought and can stand by itself as a sentence. A **dependent clause** cannot stand alone. It depends upon the independent clause of the sentence to complete its meaning. Dependent clauses start with words like *who, which, that, because, when, if, until, before,* and *after*.

dependent clause — independent clause
When we went to the school carnival, we witnessed many pranks.

Draw a line from each independent clause to a dependent clause to form a new sentence.

Independent clause	Dependent clause
The teacher fell into the dunk tank	because she had a "kick-me" sign stuck to her back.
Her face turned bright red	after their canoe was tipped over.
The pie hit her in the face	when the baseball hit the target.
After he fell asleep,	they sprayed shaving cream all over his head.
All the girls screamed	while he was not looking.
He was so embarrassed	when she saw her undies being strung up the flagpole.
They put a worm on his plate	that he couldn't speak.
Everyone laughed	when he threw it.

The sentences below each have a dependent and an independent clause. Underline the dependent clause once and the independent twice.

1. Janie was sad because she didn't have enough money to go on the Ferris wheel.
2. After Jack ate two bags of cotton candy, he felt sick.
3. While Mrs. Brown wasn't looking, two kids snuck into the Tunnel O' Love.
4. The girls all cheered when the carnival strongman lifted two grown men over his head.

Page 76

Claws

An **adjective clause** is a dependent clause that functions as an adjective. It can modify any noun or pronoun in a sentence. Adjective clauses tell *which one, what kind,* or *how many.*

*Some of the animals **that live in the wild** have claws.*

In each of the following sentences, underline each adjective clause and circle the word it modifies.

1. Feline claws, which are used to catch prey, are retractable.
2. An owl's claws, which are called talons, are dangerous weapons.
3. Rather than claws, orangutans possess fingers that have fingerprints much like a human's.
4. A polar bear uses his front paws and short, sharp claws for holding on to prey that is slippery.
5. There are five fingers on a panda's hand and five toes on each foot, which all have long, sharp claws.
6. Playful lion cubs, who must learn to hunt, use their claws to snag anything that moves.
7. The hoof of a giraffe, which has no claws, makes a print larger than a dinner plate.
8. The fishing bat, which hunts fish swimming near the water's surface, swoops down and uses its long claws to grab the fish.
9. With her back legs, the female turtle digs a hole that she will use to protect her eggs.
10. A parrot has two toes that point forward and two toes that point backward.
11. Wolf babies are born underground in dens that are often dug by the wolves' parents.
12. Claws that are found on the feet of birds, reptiles, and mammals are often sharp, hooked structures.
13. A dog's toenails, which grow long, need to be cut regularly.
14. All claws, nails, talons, horns, and hoofs are made of the same material, which is hardened cells of the epidermis, the outer layer of skin.

Page 77

Santa Claus

An **adverb clause** is a dependent clause that functions as an adverb. It can modify a verb, an adjective, or another adverb. Adverb clauses tell *how, where, when,* or *why* an action happened.

*It seems nearly everyone believes in Santa **when they are very young.***

In each of the following sentences, underline the adverb clause, circle the word or phrase it modifies, and write the question it answers: *how, when, where,* or *why.*

when 1. Santa arrives on Christmas Eve.
how 2. Santa flies with the speed of light.
how 3. Santa enters the room by coming down the chimney with a bound.
how or where 4. On his back, he carries a bag full of toys.
where 5. Up on the rooftop, the reindeer wait.
where 6. Santa sits by the fireplace and reads a note the children left.
when 7. Before getting to work, he enjoys the cookies and milk.
why 8. Santa didn't eat dinner because he knew there would be a lot of cookies tonight.
when 9. After he eats the cookies, he will give the carrots to his reindeer.
where 10. The children are fast asleep in their beds.
why 11. Because the children have been good all year, Santa will leave their favorite toys.
how 12. Santa opens his pack by untying it.
why 13. Since some of the children have been naughty, Santa must check his list.
why 14. Because they have been bad, Santa fills some children's stockings with coal.
how 15. Then, with a twinkle in his eye, he fills the others' stockings with candy and toys.
when 16. When he is finished, he lays his finger aside his nose, gives a nod, and goes.

Page 78

Window-Washing Entrepreneurs

A **noun clause** is a dependent clause that functions as a noun. It may be used as a subject, a direct object, an indirect object, an object of a preposition, or a predicate noun.

***subject**: **What occurred** was not planned at all.*
***direct object**: They wondered **what they should do** now.*
***indirect object**: Should they make **whoever broke the window** pay the bill?*
***object of the preposition**: They were grateful to **whoever would clean up the mess**.*
***predicate noun**: The good thing was **that no one was hurt**.*

In each of the following sentences, underline the noun clause and indicate how the clause is used in the sentence: **S** (subject), **DO** (direct object), **IO** (indirect object), **OP** (object of a preposition), or **PN** (predicate noun).

DO 1. Felix and Frank considered what they could do to earn money.
DO 2. Felix thought that his idea might work.
S 3. What Felix proposed was to start their own window-washing business.
S 4. That people would want their windows cleaned seemed obvious to Frank.
PN 5. How to get the proper equipment was what they had to figure out first.
DO 6. Then, whatever they could promise to persuade their customers they printed in their advertisement fliers.
IO 7. They would give whoever called in the first week a discount price.
DO 8. Felix and Frank agreed that the fliers should be hand-delivered.
PN 9. Their initial week of washing windows was pretty much what they expected.
S 10. Whoever had the dirtiest windows seemed to call for service.
S 11. That you should keep your word was their business motto.
IO 12. So, Felix and Frank gave whoever called a 50 percent discount that first week.
OP 13. Throughout the summer, they continued to work hard for whomever they could.
S 14. That they made some money is certainly true.
OP 15. They finished the summer feeling proud of that which they had accomplished.

Page 79

Masterpiece in the Snow

An **adjective clause** is a dependent clause that functions as an adjective by telling *what kind* or *which one*. An **adverb clause** is a dependent clause that functions as an adverb. It can modify verbs, adjectives, or other adverbs, and tells *where, when, in what manner, to what extent, under what condition,* or *why*. A **noun clause** is a dependent clause that functions as a noun.

*adjective clause: Building a snowman is one pastime **that we enjoy each winter.***
*adverb clause: We dress warmly **when we play in the snow.***
*noun clause: **What we create out of the snow** is always a labor of love.*

In each of the following sentences, underline the dependent clause and indicate if it is an adjective (ADJ), an adverb (ADV), or a noun (N) clause.

ADJ 1. We didn't want to build a snowman that was like all the others.
N 2. Every winter we do that.
ADJ 3. Today we would create a snowman that no one would forget.
N 4. What Craig thought of was perfect!
N 5. Build a giant snow monster is what we would do.
ADV 6. The monster grew quickly because the snow packed so well.
ADJ 7. The neighbor who lives next door brought a six-foot ladder.
N 8. What became the monster's body were packed, giant snowballs.
ADV 9. He grew taller after we hoisted the second ball on top of the first.
ADV 10. To build his height, we added buckets of snow.
ADV 11. Since we were building a giant snow monster, we wanted him to be at least eight feet tall.
ADV 12. When the mound of snow was big enough, we carved out his face and his limbs.
ADV 13. When we stood back and looked, everyone agreed that he wasn't finished.
N 14. What he needed was sharp teeth and beady eyes.
ADV 15. Finally, we turned our snowy monster green by spraying him with colored water.
ADJ 16. The snow monster that we put so much hard work into is a masterpiece.

Page 80

So Many Sweets

Noun Clauses

In each of the following sentences, underline the noun clause and indicate how the clause is being used in the sentence: S (subject), DO (direct object), IO (indirect object), OP (object of the preposition), or PN (predicate noun).

PN 1. Frosted cookies are what make Christmas delicious.
S 2. Whoever made this chocolate pie should be kissed.
DO 3. I hope that this caramel corn isn't stale.
IO 4. Meg will give whoever says please a giant candy bar.
OP 5. The cotton candy stuck to all of her fingers.

Adjective Clauses

In each of the following sentences, underline the adjective clause and circle the word it modifies.

1. We buy ice cream from the man who drives the ice-cream truck.
2. The honey that the bees make tastes great on toast.
3. His jawbreaker, which was the size of a golf ball, lasted a long time.
4. Dad and I get doughnuts at the bakery where my cousin works.
5. The fudge maker who worked in town was known for his delicious candy.

Adverb Clauses

In each of the following sentences, underline the adverb clause and write the question it answers: *how, when, where,* or *why*

when 1. You should brush your teeth whenever you've eaten sweets.
why 2. My brother is hyperactive because he ate too much Halloween candy.
when 3. At Christmastime, we dip candy canes in melted chocolate.
how 4. We fondue by dipping strawberries in melted chocolate too.
where 5. Lisa and Mike shared a malted milkshake at the ice-cream parlor.

Page 81

A Bag of Bones

An **appositive** is a noun or noun phrase placed next to or very near another noun or noun phrase to identify, explain, or supplement its meaning, or to rename the initial noun or pronoun.

Bones, the scaffolding of the body, are tied together with ligaments.

Underline the appositives in each sentence. There may be more than one appositive in each.

1. The cranium, or brain case, is made up of five bones.
2. The clavicle, or collarbone, is a slender, rodlike bone that acts like a brace for the shoulder blade.
3. The shoulder blades, or scapulae, are broad, triangle-shaped bones located on either side of the upper back.
4. A person's breastbone, the sternum, is a flat, elongated bone.
5. Each upper limb of a person's body consists of an upper arm bone, the humerus, and two lower arm bones, the radius and the ulna.
6. Your wrist, or carpus, is composed of eight small carpal bones that are firmly connected in two rows of four bones each.
7. Phlanges, finger and toe bones, play an important role in the body.
8. While in-line skating, John hurt his patella, his knee cap, when he collided with a parked car.
9. The lower leg is formed by two bones, the large tibia and the slender fibula, which extend from the knee to the ankle.
10. The longest bone in the body, the femur, extends from the hip to the knee.
11. Did you know that the seven tarsals that form the heel and the back part of the instep create the tarsus, or the ankle?
12. The smallest bones in the entire body, the malleus, incus, and stapes, connect the eardrum to the inner ear and transmit vibrations from the outer ear to the inner ear.

Page 82

That's Amoré!

A **sentence** expresses a complete thought. A sentence must contain a subject and a predicate. Every sentence begins with a capital letter and ends with a period, a question mark, or an exclamation mark.

***complete sentence:** My sister eats pizza in bed.*
***incomplete sentence:** Pizza in bed.*

Read each sentence below. Before each, write **C** if it is a complete sentence or write **NC** if it is not a complete sentence. If you wrote NC, rewrite the incomplete sentences to create complete ones.

C 1. It is my turn to make dinner for my family.
C 2. Pizza is it!
NC 3. First, the dough for the crust. First, I make the dough for the crust.
C 4. We like it thick.
C 5. I spread the dough evenly into the deep-dish pan.
NC 6. Add Grandma's homemade sauce. I add Grandma's homemade sauce.
C 7. It is delicious.
NC 8. One cup ham, one cup green pepper, and two cups pineapple. Then I put one cup ham, one cup green pepper, and two cups pineapple on top.
C 9. Don't forget the mozzarella.
NC 10. Lots of cheese on top. I put lots of cheese on top, too.
C 11. Bake it.
C 12. After thrity mintues at 375°, it is perfect.
C 13. Now we'll eat and enjoy.
NC 14. Cold pop a must too. Cold pop is a must, too.
C 15. If there are any leftovers, we will have the rest for breakfast—cold!

Page 83

A Sour Experience

> The **simple subject** names the person or the object the sentence is about, not including modifying words such as articles (a, an, the) or adjectives. The **simple predicate** tells what the subject is or what the subject does. It is a verb or a verb phrase minus any modifying words.
>
> (simple subject) (simple predicate)
>
> *A happy kid munched on sour apples.*
>
> (simple subject) (simple predicate)
>
> *Mrs. Haggly is taking the apple trees away.*

Read the story. Underline the simple subject and circle the simple predicate in each sentence.

The apple trees along Mrs. Haggly's driveway tempted us. From our own yard, we could smell the tartness in the crisp autumn air. Shiny green apples decorated the gnarled old trees. We strained our necks to see them better. Just the thought of biting into one of those apples made our mouths water uncontrollably.

Mrs. Haggly was our only problem. Everyone knew that she was dangerous. She had long wavy white hair and a crooked face. She bent over, using a cane for balance. Many people thought she might even be a witch.

One morning, we decided to make a run for the apples. Boy was that exciting! My brother ran first. I followed. Before we knew it, we had a handful of perfect, little, green apples. Back over the fence we went quicker than ever! Exhausted and sweating beads of fear, we ate the green apples under the shade of our own tree. They were perfectly sour and delicious!

However, we paid the price for our adventure. Ohhh, did we ache! Our stomachs grew big like watermelons. We were sick all day. This story has a moral. Little green apples are sometimes wicked. Old ladies with canes are usually not.

Page 84

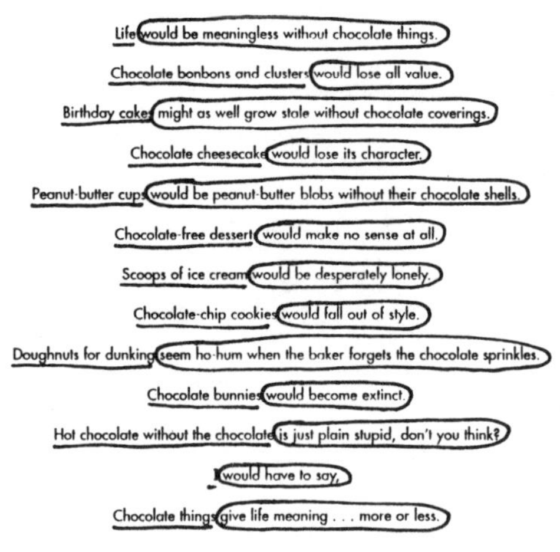

Ode to Chocolate

> The **complete subject** of a sentence tells what or who the sentence is about and may be one word or many words. The **complete predicate** tells what the subject is or does and may be one word or many words. Both the complete subject and predicate contain articles and modifying words or phrases.
>
> (complete subject) (complete predicate)
>
> *A cold glass of milk tastes great after a chocolate-chip cookie.*

In each sentence below, underline the complete subject and circle the complete predicate.

Life would be meaningless without chocolate things.

Chocolate bonbons and clusters would lose all value.

Birthday cakes might as well grow stale without chocolate coverings.

Chocolate cheesecake would lose its character.

Peanut-butter cups would be peanut-butter blobs without their chocolate shells.

Chocolate-free dessert would make no sense at all.

Scoops of ice cream would be desperately lonely.

Chocolate-chip cookies would fall out of style.

Doughnuts for dunking seem ho-hum when the baker forgets the chocolate sprinkles.

Chocolate bunnies would become extinct.

Hot chocolate without the chocolate is just plain stupid, don't you think?

I would have to say,

Chocolate things give life meaning . . . more or less.

Page 85

Autumn and Apples

> A **compound subject** is made of two or more subjects that have the same verb and are joined by a conjunction such as *and* or *or*. A **compound predicate** is two or more predicates that have the same subject and are joined by a conjunction.
>
> (compound subject) (compound predicate)
>
> *My sister and I love to make and eat caramel apples.*

Underline the compound portion in each of the following sentences. Write CS in the blank if it is a compound subject; write CP if it is a compound predicate.

CS 1. In the fall, my sister and I always make caramel apples.
CP 2. First, we pick the apples and wash them well.
CS 3. Then, Tami and I melt the caramel squares in the double boiler.
CP 4. If we do not stir the caramels well enough, the mixture will be too chunky and will not work.
CP 5. While we work, Kenneth, our younger brother, eats an apple or sneaks some caramels.
CP 6. Finally, Tami starts dipping and turning the first apple in the hot caramel.
CS 7. Mom and Dad like chopped nuts on their apples.
CP 8. I roll a few apples in the nuts and leave some plain.
CP 9. After dinner, our family will devour and enjoy them for dessert.
CP 10. We love to make caramel apples but hate to clean up the sticky mess and put away all the dishes.

In the following sentences, turn the subject into a compound subject and write the new sentence on the line. You may have to change the verb as well. SAMPLE ANSWERS

1. September is a good time to pick apples.
   September and October are good times to pick apples.
2. Deer like to eat apples.
   Deer and squirrels like to eat apples.

In the following sentences, turn the predicate into a compound predicate and write the new sentence on the line.

1. Grandma makes apple muffins.
   Grandma makes apple muffins and bakes apple pies.
2. Rotten apples give me a stomachache.
   Rotten apples give me a stomachache and make me sick.

Page 86

Homework

> There are 4 kinds of sentences: **declarative**, **interrogative**, **imperative**, and **exclamatory**.
>
> - **Declarative** sentences make a statement and end with a period.
> - **Interrogative** sentences ask a question and end with a question mark.
> - **Imperative** sentences command or make a request and end with a period or an exclamation point. ("You" is often the implied subject of the command or request.)
> - **Exclamatory** sentences make either a statement or a command with strong feeling and end with an exclamation point.
>
> *declarative: Marcie helps Anne finish her math assignment.*
> *interrogative: Does Mike know how to divide decimals?*
> *imperative: Please ask him yourself.*
> *exclamatory: I need an answer right now!*

Label the following sentences: D (declarative), IN (interrogative), IM (imperative), or E (exclamatory). Add the correct punctuation to the end of each sentence.

Periods and exclamation points may vary slightly.

D 1. My teachers always give me too much homework.
IN 2. Don't they know I already have enough to do?
IM 3. Mow the lawn.
D 4. That's what my dad always says.
IN 5. Did you take out the trash?
D 6. My mom always wants me to empty the trash cans and take them out to the curb.
D 7. Sometimes I even have to help my brother with his paper route.
IM 8. Just imagine how tired I get.
E 9. Can't a guy get a break!
D 10. Mrs. Barts wants me to do a report about Egyptian mummies, and Mr. Lee suggests I study for the algebra test.
IN 11. What do I know about mummies anyway?
IM 12. Give me a hand with this algebra.
D 13. I just remembered that I have to rake my grandma's leaves tonight.
E 14. I've got too much homework!
D 15. The basketball game is on.

Page 87

Shaq

Declarative sentences can be changed to form interrogative sentences.

The basketball is a dull shade of orange.
What color is the basketball?

Shaquille O'Neal is the slam-dunking star center for the Orlando Magic. Shaq's full name is Shaquille Rashaun O'Neal. His name means "little warrior." Shaquille was born on March 6, 1972. When he was growing up, his parents taught him to value a strong work ethic, wisdom, and responsibility. Shaq's father introduced him to the game of basketball to reinforce these values. Many years later, Shaq went to Louisiana State University to study and to play basketball. He was 17 years old when he began playing college basketball. At that time, he was seven feet one inch (2.2 m) tall and he weighed 290 (132 kg) pounds. Just three years later, Shaq turned pro. The Orlando Magic won the chance to draft him. He began playing in the NBA in 1992.

Change each declarative sentence into an interrogative one.

1. Who is Shaquille O'Neal?
2. What is Shaq's full name?
3. What does his name mean?
4. When was Shaquille born?
5. What did his parents teach him when he was growing up?
6. How did Shaq's father reinforce these values?
7. Where did Shaq go to study and play basketball?
8. How old was he when he began playing college basketball?
9. What size was he at that time?
10. When did Shaq turn pro?
11. Which team won the chance to draft him?
12. When did he begin playing in the NBA?

Page 88

Sumo

A **simple sentence** contains one independent clause. (An independent clause contains a subject and a predicate and can stand alone.) A **compound sentence** contains two independent clauses that are closely related. A comma and conjunction or a semicolon usually connects the two clauses.

Maxwell is a sumo wrestler. (simple sentence)
Maxwell trains very hard, but he has never won a competition. (compound sentence)

Put an S on the line in front of each simple sentence and a C on the line in front of each compound sentence.

S 1. Sumo is the national sport of Japan.
C 2. There are six major sumo tournaments held each year in Japan, and they attract the attention of the entire nation.
S 3. In Japan, a tournament is called a *basho.*
S 4. A sumo ring measures 12 feet (3.66m) in diameter and is made of sand and clay.
S 5. The goal in sumo wrestling is to either throw your opponent to the ground or to force him out of the ring.
C 6. Sumo has no weight classes for competition, and many wrestlers weigh more than 350 pounds (159kg).
C 7. The wrestler's big stomach provides him a low center of gravity, and it helps him withstand a charge by his opponent.
S 8. Every sumo competition begins with a religious-type ceremony.
C 9. Before each match, the competitors clap their hands to awaken the gods, they throw salt into the ring to purify the ground, and they stamp their feet to crush evil.
S 10. When the referee gives the signal, the wrestlers take their positions.
S 11. They crouch down and place both hands in front of them with their knuckles on the ground.
S 12. The highest rank in sumo wrestling is *yokozuna,* which means "grand champion."

Page 89

Butterflies

A **complex sentence** contains an independent clause and one or more dependent clauses. An **independent clause** contains a subject and a predicate and can stand alone. A **dependent clause** has a subject and a predicate, but it cannot stand by itself and still make sense. A dependent clause often begins with a relative pronoun such as *who, which, that, whose,* or *whom.*

independent clause: *The butterfly flitted from flower to flower.*
dependent clause: *whose wings were brightly colored*
complex sentence: *The butterfly, whose wings were brightly colored, flitted from flower to flower.*

Underline the dependent clauses in the sentences below.

1. The butterfly, which is a cousin to the moth, can be seen near flowerbeds during the day.
2. Butterflies, whose bodies are partly covered with multicolored scales, have six legs, four wings, and two antennae.
3. Because of many rows of scales, the butterfly has beautifully colored wings with fantastic designs.
4. The eye of a butterfly, which is made up of thousands of tiny lenses, sees color and movement very well.
5. The two antennae, which are located on the top of its head, are the smell sensors of the butterfly.
6. Because the butterfly is often in search of nectar, it flies from flower to flower.
7. While it searches for nectar, the butterfly performs an important job.
8. It carries pollen from one flower to another, which helps the flowers reproduce.
9. Butterfly caterpillars have mouth parts, which they use to chew leaves and other plant parts.
10. Because they damage crops, some kinds of caterpillars are considered pests.
11. Butterflies have a hard skin called the exoskeleton, which supports the body and protects the internal organs.
12. A butterfly that emits the appropriate scent during mating will be accepted immediately as a mate.

Page 90

A Day at Camp

A **complex sentence** contains one independent clause and one or more dependent clauses. The dependent clause may interrupt the independent clause, as in the second example below.

We look forward to going to camp every year because we have so much fun.
Our favorite camp, which is way up north, is open all summer long.

Draw a double line under the dependent clauses and a single line under the independent clauses.

6:45 A.M.	When the bugle plays at 6:45 A.M., all campers will rise.
7:00 A.M.	Because physical fitness is essential, a one-mile run is required.
7:30 A.M.	The showers, which are centrally located, will be available for use.
8:00 A.M.	Breakfast, which is always served promptly at 8:00 A.M., will be nutritious.
8:45 A.M.	Each camper is responsible for washing his own dishes because he will use them again at lunch.
9–11:30 A.M.	Morning activities, which include hiking, canoeing, and archery, will be open to everyone.
11:30–noon	Camper's awards will be presented to individuals when we gather for lunch.
Noon	Because everyone will be hungry, we will have a hearty lunch.
1:00–3:00 P.M.	Sign up for your favorite arts and crafts classes because space in each class is limited.
3:00–4:00 P.M.	We will swim each afternoon, whenever the weather cooperates.
5:00 P.M.	Camp cooks, who have prepared your evening meal, will dish it out at 5:00 P.M.
6:00 P.M.	When dinner is done, campers will be encouraged to perform skits.
7:00 P.M.	Scavenger hunts and games, which should be challenging, will begin.
8:00 P.M.	When there is no rain, we will sit around the campfire and sing songs.
9:00 P.M.	Because the bugle will blare early tomorrow, everyone must go to sleep.

Page 91

Who Am I?

A **compound–complex sentence** contains two or more independent clauses and at least one dependent clause.

When you read the clues, you will begin to identify the mystery animal, and you will make your guess.

In these compound–complex sentences, underline the independent clauses once and the dependent clauses twice. Can you guess what animal this is?

1. Because the weather is turning cold, I will go south, and I will join others like myself.
2. I can weigh more than ten elephants, and when I am fully grown, my length is greater than a four-story building.
3. Scientists, who are called cetologists, know we have black and white markings, but that our markings differ from one another.
4. Though we all have similar markings, our individual ones are just as unique as a person's fingerprints, and they are as individual as a giraffe's spots.
5. I have a big tail, and I like to flip it up when I am traveling.
6. My skin, which covers my entire body, is smooth and hairless, but it is bumpy on parts of my head.
7. Although I eat huge amounts of food, I have no teeth, instead I have baleens.
8. If I rise out of the water, you might see my dorsal fins, or I might show you a glimpse of my tail.
9. Underneath my skin is a thick layer of dense fatty tissue, which is called blubber, and it maintains my body temperature at 93–99° F (34–37° C).
10. When I exhale, a jet of steam emerges from the top of my head, and it is released through a blowhole.
11. I communicate using a variety of moans and screams, and when I am mating, I use a special pattern of these, called "songs."

Page 92

Soup's On

A **simple sentence** contains one independent clause. A **compound sentence** is made of two independent clauses connected by a comma and conjunction. A **complex sentence** includes one independent clause and one or more dependent clauses. A **compound–complex sentence** contains two or more independent clauses (connected by a comma and conjunction) and at least one dependent clause.

simple: I like soup.
compound: I like soup, and I prefer it hot.
complex: When I get home from school, I like soup.
compound-complex: When I get home from school, I like soup, and I prefer it hot.

Identify the following sentences as S (simple), C (compound), CX (complex), or C-CX (compound–complex).

C 1. My grandma makes the best cheesy broccoli soup, and she serves it with homemade bread.
S 2. Big chunks of potatoes make potato soup worth eating.
CX 3. Even though I hate pea soup, my mom always makes it.
S 4. Chili tastes great on a cold winter day.
C-CX 5. Because we eat soup every Saturday night, we try lots of kinds, and we serve them in a variety of ways.
CX 6. When we go out for Chinese food, we usually order egg drop soup.
CX 7. In my opinion, a black bean soup with a rice and tomato salsa on top is the ultimate best.
C-CX 8. If you come over tonight, you may stay for dinner, and we will share our minestrone.
S 9. Dad loves venison stew and whole wheat rolls.
C 10. Some people like clam chowder, but I'm not crazy about it.
CX 11. When we're in a hurry, we just open a can of chicken noodle.
C-CX 12. Kyle likes to eat at the Souper Bowl, where we go for soup and sandwiches, and he always orders their famous onion soup.

Page 93

The Rodeo

A group of words punctuated like a sentence but not containing a complete thought is called a **fragment**. A fragment frequently lacks a subject or a predicate. Sometimes, a fragment may be corrected by adding a word or words. Other times, the correction is made by connecting the fragment to a preceding or following sentence and changing the punctuation.

fragment: After the show.
correct: After the show, the audience exploded with applause.
fragment: One of the reasons I could not do my homework.
correct: One of the reasons I could not do my homework is that I went to the rodeo.

Correct each of the fragments by connecting it to a "partner" sentence or group of words. Write the correct letter on the line. If the sentence is not a fragment, write OK on the line.

A. bareback riders use	D. great North American sport	G. he gets bucked off
B. entertain the crowd	E. doesn't use a saddle	H. is thrilling
C. untamed horses	F. bull riding	

E 1. A bareback bronco rider.
D 2. For over 150 years, rodeo has been a.
B 3. At the rodeo, bucking broncos and their riders.
OK 4. Riders mount in a stall called a chute.
A 5. A leather handle called a rigging to hang on to.
H 6. The eight second ride.
OK 7. The cowboy tries to stay on the horse.
C 8. Will try to toss a rider off.
OK 9. Then the pick-up man helps.
F 10. Is truly the most dangerous event.
G 11. If he can't hang on.
OK 12. A clown distracts it.

Page 94

By the Shore

A **run-on sentence** consists of two or more complete sentences written without proper punctuation between them. Run-ons can be corrected in three ways.

1. If the two sentences are closely related, they can be separated by a semi-colon.
   Shells are very pretty; they make especially good necklaces.
2. Closely related sentences can also be separated with a comma and a conjunction.
   I like all kinds of fish, but angel fish are my favorite.
3. Sentences that are not closely related can be separated with a period.
   Puffer fish are funny-looking. They live in salt water.

Correct the run-ons below by adding the proper punctuation and conjunctions if necessary. If a sentence is not a run-on, write OK on the line.

____ 1. The moray eel conceals himself by hiding in the rocks; he pops his head out to catch his prey.
OK 2. A group of sea animals named sea squirts shoot water through one of two body openings.
____ 3. Starfish and sea urchins have no heads, but they have mouths on their bellies.
____ 4. Starfish have five flexible arms, and they use them to walk around.
____ 5. A seahorse is a fish that swims in an upright position. The male has a kangaroo-like pouch that holds the fertilized eggs until they hatch.
____ 6. Most sea urchins are vegetarians or scavengers. Most are equipped with five sharp teeth for scraping food.
____ 7. Sand dollars are shallow-water echinoderms. Their bodies are covered with spines which aid in locomotion.
OK 8. Seaweed is commonly found along rocky beaches because it grows attached to the rocks.
OK 9. Female sea turtles come ashore to lay their eggs in holes, which they dig and then cover with sand.
____ 10. A sea otter's hind feet are broadened into flippers; his forefeet are useful for grasping.
OK 11. The sea cucumber, a type of sea animal with a long, fleshy body, belongs to the echinoderm group.
____ 12. Gulls are long-winged birds. They are often seen flying and dipping over large bodies of water.

Page 95

Monster Mile

Rewrite the article below, correcting the run-ons, fragments, and stringy sentences.

Suggested revisions

Seeker's Thrill amusement park has just released news that the world's most state-of-the-art roller coaster, the new Monster Mile, is ready to roll.

A select group of roller coaster enthusiasts will be the first to experience the ride. It is expected to be a sunny day at the park. The 100 special guests will strap-in at 9:00 A.M. The ride will exceed record roller coaster speeds. Riders of the Monster Mile will stand during their 4.5 minute race through fifteen corkscrew loops, dozens of turns, and a mile of coaster track. Other roller coasters will not be running until the park opens. The park will be open to the public at 12:00 noon, and the rides will run until 11:00 P.M. Parking will be free all day. Guests at Seeker's Thrill will be rewarded with a complimentary Monster Mile ice-cream bar after riding the thrilling roller coaster. Some may choose not to ride the foreboding giant. Before leaving the park, however, anyone can purchase an "I survived the Monster Mile" t-shirt or hat. There will be a fireworks finale at 11:00 P.M. Seeker's Thrill will close at midnight on its grand opening day, so have a great time and go "the Monster Mile!"

Page 96

In the Dohyo

Choppy sentences are a series of short, closely related sentences that, if joined together, could be made into one smoother and less repetitive sentence.

choppy sentences: *This book is interesting. It is a story about sumo wrestling. It is an exciting story.*

corrected sentence: *This book is an interesting and exciting story about sumo wrestling.*

Rewrite the choppy sentences below into smooth, non-repetitive sentences.

1. In Japan, sumo wrestlers are considered living icons. They are heroes of their national sport.
   In Japan, sumo wrestlers are considered living icons and heroes of their national sport.
2. Sumo wrestlers prefer to be extremely large. Wrestlers strive to get very fat.
   Sumo wrestlers prefer to be extremely large, and they strive to get very fat.
3. A tournament lasts for fifteen days. Wrestlers face a different opponent each day.
   A tournament lasts for fifteen days, and wrestlers face a different opponent each day.
4. Wrestlers throw a handful of purifying salt. They must do this. They throw the salt before entering the hallowed ring.
   Wrestlers must throw a handful of purifying salt before entering the hallowed ring.
5. The wrestling ring is considered a sacred place. It is called a *dohyo*.
   The wrestling ring, called a dohyo, is considered a sacred place.
6. Most matches are short. Most are intense. Most last less than one minute.
   Most matches are short and intense, and most last less than one minute.
7. There is an important factor in sumo wrestling. Mental strength is important. It often provides the winning edge.
   Mental strength is an important factor in sumo wrestling that often provides the winning edge.
8. Slapping is allowed. Pushing is allowed. Tripping is allowed. Punching with the fist is not allowed.
   Slapping, pushing, and tripping are allowed, but punching with the fist is not allowed.

Page 97

After the Beep, Leave Your Message

A **comma** is used to set off an introductory phrase or dependent clause.
After a big day of sledding and skating, we made hot cocoa.

A **comma** is used after words of direct address at the beginning of a sentence.
Jodie, did you bring the marshmallows?

A **comma** is used after introductory words, such as, *yes, indeed, well, in addition to, thus*, and *moreover*.
Yes, I did.

Use two **commas** to set off interrupting words or expressions.
The marshmallows, I think, are a bit stale.

Place commas in the phone messages below.

- Hi, call me when you get home. I will, I think, be home all evening.
- Greg, I miss you. In addition to that, I've got something exciting to tell you.
- Since you're not home yet, I think I'll go shopping without you. By the way, I did find your bracelet.
- Mom, I went to Scott's. Yes, I already did all of my English homework.
- Laura, I received your request. For more information, write to the Tennessee Tourist Association.
- Hello, is this the Lewis residence? Your dog, I believe, is running loose on Jasper Court.
- Don't forget your dentist appointment, Mr. Bean, at 11:00 A.M. tomorrow morning. If you can't make it, please call and cancel as soon as possible.
- This is Rebecca, your niece, calling at 5:00 P.M. If you still need a babysitter for Friday night, I can do it.

Page 98

Prehistoric Creatures

Use **hyphens** to

a. break a word between syllables at the end of a line in running text.
b. join two-part numbers from twenty-one to ninety-nine.
c. write a fraction as a word.
d. join some compound nouns and adjectives.

a. Some scientists claim that dinosaurs roamed the earth mill-ions of years ago.
b. thirty-five, eighty-two
c. one-fortieth, two-thirds
d. fat-necked, hurricane-like

Add a hyphen to each of the following sentences. Then, in the blank, write the letter from above to show which rule you have applied.

d 1. The woolly mammoth was an elephant-like animal covered with long, thick hair.
a 2. The mammoths had long, curved tusks useful during the winter in clear-ing away the snow to find grass to eat.
a 3. In permafrost regions of Siberia, some mammoths have been found per-fectly preserved.
b 4. The average Stegosaurus was twenty-five feet long and weighed two to three tons.
a 5. The four sharp spikes on its tail were quite useful in wounding its ene-mies.
d 6. Triceratops, meaning "three-horned face," was an aggressive dinosaur.
d 7. It chewed large amounts of plants with its razor-sharp teeth.
c 8. Triceratops stood nine and one-half feet tall.
b 9. Tyrannosaurus, a forty-seven foot long tyrant, weighed seven tons.
a 10. Its huge jaws and sharp teeth helped make it the most pow-erful meat eater.
a 11. Brachiosaurus was an enormous herbivorous dino-saur.
b 12. It was seventy-five feet long, forty feet tall, and weighed eighty tons.

Page 99

Peter's Pizza

Quotation marks are used to enclose **direct quotation.** The end punctuation usually comes before the final quotation mark at the end of the quote. Always capitalize the first word of direct quotation. Do not capitalize the first word in the second part of an interrupted quotation unless the second part begins a new sentence.

Cameron said, "Would you like pizza for dinner?"
"Yes, that sounds good!" replied Angela. "I'll call Peter's and order one."
"After you order it," responded Cameron, "we will need to find some money."

Rewrite the following sentences by adding the correct punctuation and capitalization.

1. hello, this is Peter's Pizza how may I help you greeted Eric
   "Hello, this Peter's Pizza. How may I help you?" greeted Eric.
2. i'd like a large pizza please Angela replied
   "I'd like a large pizza, please," Angela replied.
3. What would you like on that Eric asked
   "What would you like on that?" Eric asked.
4. I'll have pepperoni and anchovies said Angela
   "I'll have pepperoni and anchovies," said Angela.
5. i'm sorry to tell you began Eric but we are out of pepperoni
   "I'm sorry to tell you," began Eric, "but we are out of pepperoni."
6. oh, that's okay Angela responded i'll just have anchovies then
   "Oh, that's okay," Angela responded. "I'll just have anchovies then."

Continue Angela's conversation with Cameron when she gets off the phone. Write 4 more sentences with direct quotation.

1. Answers will vary.
2.
3.
4.

Page 100

Gossip

A **direct quotation** is the use of someone's exact words. It is always set off with quotation marks. An **indirect quotation** is the writer's description of someone else's words. It does not require quotation marks.

direct: Brent said, "Max is bringing the dog to the vet."
indirect: Brent said that Max is bringing the dog to the vet.

For each of the following sentences, write DQ (direct quotation) or IQ (indirect quotation) on the line. Then add quotation marks wherever they are needed.

The Orange Hair

DQ 1. Jennifer asked, "Did you see Rae's hair? It is bright orange!"
DQ 2. "She dyed it herself!" added Jordan.
DQ 3. "Yeah," sneered Tamara, "she needs a wig."

The Surprise Party

DQ 1. "I'll see you at the party!" declared Paige.
DQ 2. "What party?" asked Maya.
DQ 3. "Steve's brothers are giving him a surprise birthday party," answered Paige, "and everyone is going."
IQ 4. Maya said that she would love to go, too.

The Joke

DQ 1. "Don't look now," warned Jeff, "but Robby is about to drink his pop."
DQ 2. "So what?" Anna questioned.
IQ 3. Dan told Anna about the plastic worm that they had dropped in Robby's cup.
IQ 4. Jeff then said that Robby had just spit his pop across the table.

The Romance

IQ 1. Sarah mentioned that Rachelle was crazy about Emilio.
DQ 2. "No way!" interjected Kate. "He's such a creep!"
DQ 3. "Maybe, but he's gorgeous," reminded Allison.
DQ 4. "Too bad," added Tamara, "because he likes Stacey Pool."

Page 101

In the Pool!

A **colon** is used between the hour and the minutes when time is written using numbers. A colon is also used to introduce a list or a series of things unless the series is preceded by an expression, such as, *for example, namely, for instance,* or *that is.*

School begins at 8:20 A.M. each day, Monday through Friday.
I have to take several things to school each day: my backpack, my lunch, and my house key.
*I have to take several things to school each day, **namely,** my backpack, my lunch, and my house key.*
(no colon necessary)

Write the time correctly in the blanks using numbers and colons.

9:30 My swimming class begins at nine thirty A.M. each morning.
9:35 We change into our suits and quickly shower by nine thirty-five.
9:45 If we're not sitting on the bench at the exact time, we will have five extra laps during our warm-up, which lasts for ten minutes.
10:05 Then, we practice our strokes until five after ten.
10:15 Next, we do rescue drills for ten minutes.
10:25 Diving practice follows until ten twenty-five.
10:30 Then we have just five minutes to shower and change back into our clothes.
10:40 Can you believe we have to be back to our next class by ten forty A.M.?

Punctuate these lists correctly.

1. There are several categories of swimmers: beginner, intermediate, and advanced.
2. Many of my classmates are excellent divers, namely, Pete, Carlos, Susan, Amanda, and Yong.
3. Every day I take a bag of items to class: swimsuit, shampoo, hairbrush, and deodorant.
4. Today we practiced some strokes, for example, the breaststroke, backstroke, and butterfly.
5. In the locker room, there is a huge pile of towels of all colors: green, blue, red, orange, and purple.
6. After swimming, I still have four more classes, that include, Algebra, English, General Science, and Band.

Page 102

The History of the World

A **semicolon** is used to join two independent clauses that are closely related if a conjunction is not used. (An **independent clause** is a group of words that could stand as a complete sentence by itself.)

The Olympic Games originated in ancient Greece; Greek gods were important to the people of Greece.
(incorrect, these sentences are not closely related.)
The Olympic Games originated in ancient Greece; the main event was the pentathlon.
(correct, these sentences are closely related.)

Determine whether the following sentences are joined correctly. Write **Yes** on the line if they are; write **No** if they are not.

Y 1. The Phoenicians were the most famous traders of the ancient world; they traded papyrus, ivory, glass, and wool.
N 2. The Persians built roads and canals; Alexander the Great's army defeated them.
Y 3. Hittite rulers signed some of the first treaties; treaties helped to bring about peace.
N 4. Egyptian writing was based in hieroglyphics; the Egyptians worshipped many gods.
Y 5. Ancient Greece was divided into city states; Athens and Sparta were rivals.
Y 6. Roman citizens were separated into two classes; the plebeians were commoners, and the patricians were nobles.
Y 7. Charlemange was a great ruler and warrior during medieval times; his kingdom extended over most of western Europe.
N 8. King John became king of England in 1199; he signed the Magna Carta.
Y 9. During the Renaissance, Leonardo daVinci painted the *Mona Lisa* and *The Last Supper*; he is considered an artistic genius.
N 10. The Protestant Reformation was a religious revolt against the Roman Catholic Church; Martin Luther was a German clergyman.
Y 11. Napoleon Bonaparte created a French empire after the revolution; he ruled as a military dictator.
Y 12. The Industrial Revolution followed the Enlightenment; it was a time when power-driven machinery began to replace manual labor.
Y 13. World War I started in 1914; it was considered the war to end all wars.
Y 14. A world wide depression occurred in the 1930s; many people lost their jobs and their homes.

Page 103